# VEILLEUSES

## 1750-1860

# VEILLEUSES

## 1750 - 1860

### by Harold Newman

South Brunswick

New York: A. S. Barnes and Company

London: Thomas Yoseloff Ltd

©1967 by A. S. Barnes and Co., Inc.
Library of Congress Catalogue Card Number: 66-18198


A. S. Barnes and Co., Inc.
South Brunswick, New Jersey


Thomas Yoseloff Ltd
18 Charing Cross Road
London W.C. 2, England


6494
Printed in the United States of America

# Acknowledgments

The reproduction of the photographs shown in the Plates and Figures of this book has been made with the consent and through the courtesy of the respective museums and private collectors who own the pieces and by whom all further reproduction rights are strictly reserved, as follows:

## Museums and Public Collections

Aylesbury, England: The National Trust, Waddesdon Manor. Pl. I.

Barnard Castle, Durham, England: Bowes Museum. Fig. 35.

Basel, Switzerland: Historisches Museum. Figs. 83, 87, 88, 118.

Berne, Switzerland: Kocher Collection, Historisches Museum. Fig. 76.

Brussels, Belgium: Musées Royaux d'Art et d'Histoire. Fig. 81.

Cologne, Germany: Kunstgewerbemuseum. Fig. 77.

Darmstadt, Germany: Prinz-Georg-Palais. Fig. 86.

Faenza, Italy: Museo Internazionale delle Ceramiche. Fig. 96.

Hamburg, Germany: Museum für Kunst und Gewerbe. Figs. 79, 116.

Hannoversch-Münden, Germany: Heimatmuseum. Fig. 84.

Harrisburg, Pennsylvania: William Penn Memorial Museum. Fig. 121.

Leeds, England: Leeds City Art Galleries. Fig. 16.

Leeuwarden, Holland: Princessehof Museum. Fig. 18.

Leningrad, U.S.S.R.: State Hermitage Museum. Figs. 112, 113.

Limoges, France: Musée Adrien Dubouché. Fig. 42.

London, England: Victoria and Albert Museum (Crown Copyright). Figs. 7, 21, 25.

London, England: Wellcome Historical Medical Museum. Figs. 3, 17.

Merion, Pennsylvania: Buten Museum of Wedgwood. Fig. 6.

Naples, Italy: Museo "Duca di Martina" (Villa Floridiana). Fig. 90.

Norwich, England: Norwich Castle Museum. Fig. 4.

Paris, France: Musée des Arts Décoratifs. Fig. 44.

Prague, Czechoslovakia: Národní Galerie. Fig. 115.

Rosenheim, Germany. Stadtarchiv. Pl. XIII.

Segovia, Spain: Zuloaga Ceramic Exhibit. Fig. 120.

Sèvres, France: Manufacture Nationale de Sèvres. Reprint on p. 58.

Stockholm, Sweden: Nationalmuseum. Fig. 80.

Stralsund, East Germany: Kulturhistorisches Museum. Fig. 85.

Strasbourg, France: Château des Rohan (Musée de Strasbourg). Figs. 24, 28, 109.

Sturbridge, Massachusetts: Old Sturbridge Village. Fig. 33.

Toronto, Canada: Academy of Medicine (Drake Collection). Pl. II; Figs. 2, 10, 12, 13, 19.

Trenton, Tennessee: Municipal Building (Freed Collection). Figs. 43, 45, 47, 50, 52, 58, 64, 72, 73, P-8, P-9, P-15, P-17, P-18, P-20, P-22, P-23, P-29, P-32, P-33, P-34, P-41, P-42, P-45, P-46, P-58, P-59, P-62, P-68, P-69, P-71, P-73, P-77, P-78, P-79, P-80, P-83, P-88, P-89.

Treviso, Italy: Museo Civico Luigi Bailo. Fig. 103.

Turin, Italy: Museo Civico. Fig. 93. (Brosio Collection): Figs. 29, 39, 100, 104, P-10, P-13, P-26, P-35, P-36, P-39, P-48, P-51, P-53, P-56, P-57, P-61, P-65, P-66, P-67, P-70, P-81, P-82.

Venice, Italy: Museo Correr (Ca'Rezzonico). Figs. 66, 91.

Vienna, Austria: Osterreichisches Museum für angewandte Kunst. Figs. 78, 105, 110.

Williamsburg, Virginia: Colonial Williamsburg. Figs. 1, 5, 9.

Zurich, Switzerland: Schweizerische Landesmuseum. Fig. 117.

## Private Collections

M. Georges Berthelot, Paris, France: Pl. VI; Figs. 32, 49, P-7, P-40.

M. René Berthelot, Paris, France: Figs. 23, P-86.

Mr. Laurel G. Blair, Blair Museum of Lithophanes, Toledo, Ohio: Figs. 62, 63.

Broulard Collection, Baumes-les-Messieurs, Jura, France: Pls. V, VII, VIII, XI; Figs. 22, 27, 30, 31, 34, 37, 38, 41, 48, 51, 54, 56, 59, 60, 74, P-2, P-3, P-4, P-6, P-11, P-14, P-27, P-31, P-44, P-60, P-72, P-75.

Rag. Antonio Cecchetto, Nove, Italy: Fig. 106.

Dott. Mario Chiavassa, Milan, Italy: Figs. 97, 101, P-19, P-25, P-49, P-50, P-63, P-64, P-76, P-84, P-85, P-90.

Miss Elaine Denby, London, England: Fig. 8.

Gandur Collection, Orléans, France: Figs. 26, 70, 71, P-12, P-16, P-21, P-28, P-30, P-52, P-55, P-87.

Marchese Leonardo Ginori-Lisci, Florence, Italy: Fig. 108.

Mme. Raoul Kraft, Geneva, Switzerland: Pl. IX; Fig. 36.

Mrs. Nina Fletcher Little, Brookline, Massachusetts: Figs. 15, 20.

Newman Collection, Metairie, Louisiana (now in London, England): Pls. III, IV, X, XII, XIV, XV. Figs. 14, 40, 46, 53, 55, 57, 61, 65, 67, 68, 69, 75, 82, 89, 94, 98, 102, 107, 111, 114, 119, 122, P-1, P-5, P-24, P-37, P-38, P-43, P-47, P-54, P-74, P-91.

Sr. Joachim Pinto-Basto, Ilhova, Portugal: Pl. XVI.

R. S. Collection, Rome, Italy: Fig. 92.

Dott. Alberto Robiati, Milan, Italy: Fig. 95.

Mr. Donald C. Towner, London, England: Fig. 11.

# Foreword

In the field of ceramic literature there is no other book quite like this one. Monographs about factories, the productions of countries, or the more familiar types of ware exist in quantity, but this work is devoted to a particular and little-known vessel in all its aspects, combining, between the same covers, specialization with a wide view of ceramic history.

The author, Harold Newman, is one of the pioneers of veilleuse collecting, and it is now ten years since he introduced this fascinating kind of vessel to English collectors in the pages of *Apollo*. Until he called my attention to the more exotic varieties (now longer ago than either of us cares to recall), I was inclined to regard them as no more than interesting by-products of a few factories, but the author's researches and infectious enthusiasm made me realize that not the least attractive feature of the veilleuse is its universality. It was made by almost every factory, large or small, in contemporary styles which are a miniature history of the ceramic art from mid-eighteenth century onwards. They occur in pottery and porcelain, as well as in several other materials.

Beginning in the middle of the eighteenth century as food warmers, simple in form and decorated with varying degrees of elaboration, they were popularized in porcelain by the great German factories at Nymphenburg and Höchst. Soon potteries throughout Europe adapted the form into a tea warmer. When porcelain figures began to fall from favor as table decorations, henceforth to fill living room cabinets of Cousin Pons, his friends, and his successors, the art was revitalized by Jacob Petit and others who made figures ingeniously disguising tea warmers.

Purists may object and say that the veilleuse is no more than an agreeable curiosity; but how agreeable it is! The ingenuity displayed by designers is endless in its variety. That the tea warmer never became popular in nineteenth-century England is perhaps due to the English method of making tea — a spoonful for each cup and one for the pot, with freshly boiling water. This did not lend itself to the practice of keeping the liquid hot with small lamps, especially as it was apt to impart a bitter flavor to the ever-popular Indian varieties. But in the seventeenth century tea imported from China was at first made in large quantities, stored in casks, and drawn off and reheated when required. On the Continent, where China tea and other infusions were more favored, the veilleuse became a popular vessel for brewing, and it is not surprising to learn that veilleuses were made in porcelain in Moscow, presumably as a substitute for the samovar.

Harold Newman has enjoyed some special advantages denied to many of us. As the author of a popular travel guide designed to make Americans feel at home in Europe, he has been able to combine his frequent and extensive research tours with the quest for the elusive veilleuse, even in small European provincial museums and antique shops. His success in this latter field may be seen not only in his own comprehensive collection of almost every known variety but in the results of his ceramic researches now set down in permanent form as a standard work on the subject which is not likely to be superseded.

George Savage

# Preface

Fifteen years ago in Paris, upon my being shown a veilleuse for the first time and expressing complete ignorance of such objects, I was told that they might be the subject of an interesting and comparatively inexpensive collection. Having always enjoyed antique shops in an abstract way, the thought of having a specific objective in my future visits while motoring about in Europe, as I was then doing, appealed to me. Prompt investigation at some Parisian and provincial antique shops disclosed that only one in ten had a veilleuse (the others, *"Pas en ce moment"*), and that only one veilleuse in five was of interest as to form or decoration. These odds (greatly increased later as fine or rare specimens were sought) did indeed make it seem that the search would be intriguing, coupled with confirmation that prices were relatively low. So a decision was made to start a collection on a modest basis, well realizing that, as at any gambling game, the stakes would go up (they have) as the fever rose.

It was only minimum prudence then to try to learn something about veilleuses — where and when and by whom they were made. Owners of small shops were of little help, as they seldom knew the provenance of the pieces they offered. Turning to the better antique dealers for information, I fared even worse, for they scorned my inquiries with the comment that they were interested only in objects made before the nineteenth century. Later, when I could tell them of veilleuses made by leading potteries about 1760, many of them still were skeptical, so little were these pieces then known.

The libraries were my next recourse. There it soon appeared that nothing had been written on the subject, not a book or a chapter or a magazine article. Indeed, so little had been mentioned about veilleuses that such an authority on ceramics as William B. Honey could write in 1947 that the Nymphenburg food warmer was a form "not found elsewhere"! But persistent examination of many general treatises on various fields of ceramics led to an occasional reference to a food warmer or a picture of one. A search among British and Continental museums also brought to light a few fine specimens. Finally, after five years, a body of information had been collected that I included in an article published in *Apollo Magazine,* London, in 1955, with citations of a number of books that mentioned or figured veilleuses and references to some examples that had been found in museums. Since then the search has been intensified, not only in shops and auction rooms, museums and libraries, but also by correspondence with many distant museum officials and by visits to some private collectors of veilleuses who had most fortunately become known to me. Among these collectors are several who have acquired from 100 to over 500 veilleuses each. I soon realized that while many inherited individual pieces are still in European and American private homes the great bulk of surviving veilleuses, especially French ones of the nineteenth century, have become concentrated among these collectors and others still unknown to me but certainly existing.

This research established that almost every leading ceramic factory in Europe, from Chelsea to Nymphenburg, from Sèvres to Lenzburg, had made veilleuses, and that geographically they were made from Vista Alegre in Portugal to potteries near Moscow and in the Ukraine and even in Philadelphia. Among Western European countries, only Scandinavia is still not known to have made any veilleuse (except of wood), and no ceramic veilleuse from the Orient has been found. The finest examples were mainly of the period 1750-90, and specimens of these have been located in over 75 museums. Almost all the great museums in Europe and the United States have at least one eighteenth-century veilleuse, but few have more than three or four.

The scarcity of museum pieces led to the realization that, probably contrary to any other field of collecting, it would be possible to write a book mentioning every known museum specimen. While writers about the potteries of one country or about any one ceramic factory have had to select representative museum pieces to discuss or figure, and other writers in a special field such as porcelain figures or crystal paperweights or Battersea enamels likewise have had to choose specimens for the reader, here was a field where there could be an effort at full coverage of museum specimens. Of course it is realized that many examples must and do exist in museums still unknown to me, but it can be said here that every veilleuse known to me in any museum at the date of writing (about 160 pieces) is discussed in this book.

This possibility of full discussion of museum examples led to the thought that, as to the so-called *personnages* (nineteenth-century veilleuses in the form of a figure), it might also be possible to show a photograph of every known model (excluding variances of detail or of color). One hundred and one models of *personnages* are known, as contrasted with, for example, over 1,000 known Meissen figures and groups. Just as a stamp collector can look at his album and see which items are missing from his collection, so it might be made possible for an advanced collector of *personnages* to look at the figure album and know how far he had succeeded in gathering a full "set," or that he had happened upon a model not in any of the known collections and therefore likely to be rare. With the fine cooperation of the private collectors later named, it was possible to gather a set of photographs showing 91 of the 101 known models of *personnages*, and these are all included in this book together with a notation of the total number of examples of each in those collections, so that the rare models and the more common ones will be readily apparent.

I gratefully acknowledge the cooperation of the museums in Europe and the United States which not only made available for reproduction photographs of veilleuses in their collections but in numerous instances searched their storerooms to find examples not on public display. I am deeply appreciative of the assistance rendered by the many museum officials who were frequently called upon to unlock their cabinets to permit personal inspection and to answer questions regarding identification or attribution of their specimens. Among those to whom I am especially indebted are the following:

Comte J. de Borchgrave d'Altena, former Conservateur en Chef, Musées Royaux d'Art et d'Histoire, Brussels.

Dr. A. Aschl, Stadtarchiv, Rosenheim, Germany.

Dott. Gino Barioli, Director, Pinacoteca, Vicenza.

Mrs. Gail Belden, Curatorial Assistant, Henry Francis Du Pont Winterthur Museum, Winterthur, Delaware.

Mr. William A. Billington, Curator, Wedgwood Museum, Barlaston, England.

Mlle. Marcelle Brunet, Librarian, Musée de Sèvres, Sèvres.

Mrs. Yves Henry Buhler, Museum of Fine Arts, Boston, Massachusetts.

Dr. H. Bulogin, State Historical Museum, Moscow, U.S.S.R.

Mr. Harry Buten, Director, Buten Museum of Wedgwood, Merion, Pennsylvania.

Mr. Robert J. Charleston, Keeper of Ceramics, Victoria and Albert Museum, London.

Mr. Herbert C. Darbee, Curator, Old Sturbridge Village, Sturbridge, Massachusetts.

Mr. Carl C. Dauterman, Associate Curator, Metropolitan Museum of Art, New York City.

Mrs. A. Willard Duncan, Associate Curator, Colonial Williamsburg, Williamsburg, Virginia.

Prof. M. Faré, Conservateur en Chef, Musée des Arts Décoratifs, Paris.

Prof. Dott. Bianca Maria Favetta, Curator, Civici Musei di Storia ed Arte, Trieste, Italy.

Prof. H. P. Fourest, Conservateur, Musée de Sèvres, Sèvres.

Mlle. Jeanne Giacomotti, Musée du Louvre, Paris, and Musée Adrien Dubouché, Limoges.

Dr. Hans Haug, Honorary Director, Château des Rohan (Musée de Strasbourg), Strasbourg.

Dr. Dagmar Hejdová, Národní Galerie, Prague.

Dr. Carl Hernmarck, Keeper of Arts and Crafts, National Museum, Stockholm.

Dr. Gudrum Illgen, Director, Prinz-Georg-Palais, Darmstadt.

Miss M.-A. Heukensfeldt Jansen, Keeper of Ceramics, Rijksmuseum, Amsterdam.

Dr. Hermann Jedding, Director, Museum für Kunst und Gewerbe, Hamburg.

Dr. Erich Kollman, Director, Kunstgewerbemuseum, Cologne.

Dr. Hans Lanz, Curator, Historical Museum, Basel.

Dott. Giuseppe Liverani, Director, Museo Internazionale delle Ceramiche, Faenza.

Mr. Louis C. Madeira, former Associate Curator of Decorative Arts, Philadelphia Museum of Art, Philadelphia.

Prof. Giovanni Mariacher, Director, Museo Correr, Venice.

Mme. A.-M. Mariën-Dugardin, Conservateur-Adjoint, Musées Royaux, Brussels.

Dr. P. W. Meister, Director, Museum für Kunsthandwerk, Frankfurt.

Dott. Luigi Menegazzi, Director, Museo Civico Luigi Bailo, Treviso.

Mr. A. R. Mountford, Curator, City Museum and Art Gallery, Stoke-on-Trent.

Dr. Wilhelm Mrazek, Curator, Museum für angewandte Kunst, Vienna.

Dr. L. Nikiforov, State Hermitage Museum, Leningrad.

Dr. Edgar L. Pelichet, Curator, Ariana Museum, Geneva.

Sr. Luis-Felipe de Peñalosa, Zuloaga Ceramic Exhibit, Segovia.

Dr. Ernst Petrasch, Badisches Landesmuseum, Karlsruhe.

Mlle. O. Popovitch, Conservateur, Musée Céramique, Rouen.

Mlle. Monique Ray, Musée Historique, Lyons.

Dr. K. Reick, Director, Kulturhistorisches Museum, Stralsund.

Dr. Margaret Rowbottom, Wellcome Historical Medical Museum, London.

Mr. Robert Rowe, Director, City Art Galleries, Leeds.

Dr. Rainer Rückert, Director, Bavarian National Museum, Munich.

Dott. Luigi Samarati, Director, Museo Civico, Lodi.

Miss Vivian J. Scheidemantel, Associate Curator, Art Institute of Chicago, Chicago.

Dr. Rudolf Schnyder, Curator, Schweizerische Landesmuseum, Zurich.

Mrs. Josephine Setze, Yale University Museum, New Haven, Connecticut.

Mrs. Huldah M. Smith, Curator, Essex Institute, Salem, Massachusetts.

Dr. S. E. Thomas, Museum des Kunsthandwerks, Leipzig.

Dr. Pierre Verlet, Conservateur en Chef des Objets d'Art, Musée du Louvre, Paris.

Dott. Vittorio Viale, Director, Museo Civico, Turin.

Mr. Francis Watson, Director, Wallace Collection, London.

Miss Beatrice B. Wolfe, Assistant Curator, Philadelphia Museum of Art, Philadelphia.

Dr. Robert L. Wyss, Director, Historical Museum, Berne.

The library of the Victoria and Albert Museum, London, with its vast collection of books and other material on ceramics, was an essential and invaluable source of reference material, and its cooperative staff greatly facilitated my innumerable hours there.

Outstanding among the private collectors of veilleuses whose assistance was indispensable and to whom my thanks are now warmly extended are Messieurs Georges and René Berthelot, Paris, France, Sig. Mario Brosio, Rome, Italy, M. and Mme. Henri Broulard, Baumes-les-Messieurs, Jura, France, Dott. Mario Chiavassa, Milan, Italy, the late Dr. T. G. H. Drake and Mrs. Drake, Toronto, Canada, Dr. Frederick C. Freed, New York City, M. and Mme. Jacques Gandur, Orléans, France, and Mme. Raoul Kraft, Geneva, Switzerland. They all, in addition to extending an invitation to inspect their private collections in their homes, gave much time from their busy schedules to furnish details and photographs of their rare pieces.

M. Henri Broulard must be singled out for special thanks, as his enthusiastic collector's interest in veilleuses and his ever gracious and willing cooperation invariably led to prompt and helpful responses to my frequent requests for information concerning French pieces.

Many other individuals, including writers in the field of ceramics and private collectors in broader areas than veilleuses, have contributed helpful information and suggestions. Among them are the following:

Dr. Fritz Bauml, Staatliche Porzellan-Manufaktur Nymphenburg, Munich, Germany.
Mr. Laurel G. Blair, Toledo, Ohio.
Mr. Byron A. Born, New York City.
Mrs. Robert Chellis, Wellesley Hills, Massachusetts.
Marchese Leonardo Ginori-Lisci, Florence, Italy.
Mr. Geoffrey Godden, Worthing, England.
Mme. Claude de Guillebon, Paris, France.
Mr. Philip Hammerslough, New Haven, Connecticut.
Mr. Theodore Jarvis, New York City.
M. Nicolas Landau, Paris, France.
Sig. Saul Levy, Milan, Italy.
Mrs. Nina Fletcher Little, Brookline, Massachusetts.
Dr. L. Malone, General Manager, Richard-Ginori, Milan, Italy.
Sig. Mario Marenesi, Este, Italy.

Mrs. Eva R. Pinto, Northwood, England.
Sr. Joachim Pinto-Basto, Ilhova, Portugal.
Avv. Alberto Robiati, Milan, Italy.
Mr. Donald C. Towner, London, England.

I am grateful to *Apollo Magazine,* London, which in 1955 published my article on veilleuses that became the kernel of this book and whose title "Reveille for Veilleuses" has, in the ensuing ten years, been proven, by the growing interest evinced by collectors and antique dealers and by the great increase in market prices, to have been in fact prophetic.

Finally, I wish to thank Mr. George Savage, of London, England, for the many hours that he so often and so generously took from his own busy days of writing on the broader fields of English and Continental ceramics to discuss veilleuses. Above all do I appreciate his constant encouragement throughout 15 years to persevere in the research in distant museums and private collections that was essential to locate many of the heretofore unreported specimens in this thin cross section of the vast storeroom of ceramics.

H. N.

54 Cadogan Square, London.
September 1966.

# Contents

# Illustrations

ALBUM OF PERSONNAGES

# 1. Types of Veilleuses

During the 1750's, when European ceramic art was at its zenith, potters in England, France, and Germany contemporaneously began making pottery and porcelain utensils for bedside heating of sickroom and infant nourishment. Although conceived for a utilitarian purpose, they were from the beginning made by almost all the leading potteries, and the decorative modeling and coloring soon established them as attractive and prized ornaments which were sought during the ensuing 50 years by persons of wealth throughout Europe. About 1800 the warming bowl was supplanted by a teapot, influenced, no doubt, by the large ceramic kettles on warming stands that were being made during the preceding 50 years. The production and use of the ceramic tea warmer soon spread to Italy, Belgium, Switzerland, Austria, Bohemia, Russia, and Portugal, and even to the United States (Pennsylvania). Although quality of workmanship diminished, the potteries and artists vied for many decades to produce examples of unusual form and elaborate decoration, and fine specimens were made until after 1830. Production continued throughout the nineteenth century, but few pieces worthy of collectors' interest were made after 1860. From about 1830 in France ornamental use in some cases entirely superseded practical considerations as the figurine was adapted to the purpose of a tea warmer by making the piece in two sections, the upper part being a teapot and the lower part a pedestal containing the burner. All these types have now been grouped by collectors under the name *veilleuse* (pronounced *vay-euz*).

Being basically oft-used household articles, relatively few veilleuses have survived intact. There are eighteenth-century specimens in almost all the principal European and United States museums, but the bulk of the existing nineteenth-century French pieces have now been gathered together by a small group of collectors who, in the last decade or two, have found them scarce enough to whet their searching impulses and sufficiently attractive to gratify their aesthetic instincts. The collector's hope for enhancement in value has now been realized as a few writers[1] have brought the veilleuse to public attention and decorators have even created a market for modern copies.

The name *veilleuse* derives from the French *veiller,* to keep a night vigil. It originally referred to any night lamp. Only a short step was needed to apply the term to any warmer for food or drink that was to be placed at a bedside for use during the night and whose small flame afforded a bit of illumination. (Today the word *veilleuse* is still used in French and Swiss hospitals to indicate a night nurse.) In France, popular names were *chauffe-nourriture, veilleuse-tisanière,* and *veilleuse-théière.* In other European countries, appropriate prosaic names were used: in England it was a food warmer, a pap warmer, or a caudle warmer; in Germany a *Suppen-wärmer,* a *Wärmtopf,* or a *Nachtlampe mit Bouillon-kümpgen,* or more frequently a *Réchaud;* in Italy, a *bollitore,* a *scaldavivande,* a *scaldabevande,* or even (by virtue of the words painted on some pieces) a *Buona Notte.*

By whatever local name, the basic veilleuse of pottery or porcelain is a hollow pedestal (*socle*) on which sits a covered bowl (*écuelle*) or a teapot (*théière*). The bowl or teapot has a projecting bottom that fits into the pedestal and brings the contents nearer to the warming flame. To supply heat there is in the pedestal a burner, customarily a small ceramic vessel (*godet*) for oil and a floating wick (*mèche*). The complete piece is usually from 9 to 12 inches high.

The eighteenth-century food warmer with bowl is the type of veilleuse most often found in museums today. Its form is fairly standard. The pedestal is usually cylindrical or slightly conical, although some have slight curves or are baluster-shaped, pyriform, or bell-shaped. At the bottom, on one side, there is an arched aperture (half-oval or more often a cyma, tulip-shaped or other curve) so that the *godet* may be set inside. The pedestal has two side handles; the early ones are in the form of scroll knobs or masks, but some (especially English and Italian ones) have large loop handles — plain or foliated, or double interlaced bands attached by floral terminals. Above the aperture for the *godet* and also on the reverse side of the pedestal are air vents, usually decoratively hooded by masks, tassels, shells, or leaves; occasionally these hooded vents are at the sides of the pedestal instead of handles, and sometimes there are four hooded vents and no handles. Often the English and Italian pieces are further decorated with pierced designs, the most usual being the Wedgwood floral spray or imitative variations. On some pieces this piercing, which provided an illuminated pattern in addition to necessary air circulation, is very elaborate and extends entirely around the pedestal. Such pieces with piercing had no need of air vents, but vents and covering hoods or masks were often retained anyway as traditional decoration. The base of the pedestal is usually raised from the table on which it rests by means of a foot rim or slight ridge around the bottom edge.

The *godet* is a circular or rounded rectangular container, generally with one handle in the form of a horizontal leaf or a vertical loop. A few have covers. Normally the *godet* sits anywhere within the pedestal, but some models have a center position fixed by a small circular ridge or a shallow recess. Most *godets* are open vessels and merely hold oil on which floats a cork disc

with a small wick, but some are like a spirit lamp with a lid that has a central hole or small chimney for a long curled wick and other holes for air vents. A few *godets* are made of metal in the form of low spirit lamps. Candles were rarely used, as the fumes would have been unpleasant. The need for snuffing also made them impracticable. It has been recently written (but not documented) that "a small water-moistened sponge was placed within the pedestal to absorb the fumes emitted during the night and prevent their dispersal through the bedroom."[2]

The warming bowl has a projecting cylindrical or globular bottom, and is made with a flange that enables it to be partially suspended within the pedestal. There is a slight space between the lower part of the bowl and the pedestal so that circulating warm air can better heat the entire contents. Most bowls have two side handles, either flat or uplifted lateral protruberances or small loops; a few have a single handle. Many bowls have a pouring lip, in which case the cover extends in a conforming shape so as to cover the opening. In very early models, especially English ones, the cover of the bowl is surmounted by a socket for a candle so that the cover could be removed during use and the candle lit from the wick for illumination. Soon the socket was abandoned and a finial was substituted in the form of a simple knob, an acorn, a piece of fruit, a flower, or a leaf.

Some food warmers are made like a double-boiler and have an extra bowl (called in England a *liner*, in France a *bain-marie*) for hot water. This bowl is suspended by a flanged edge within the pedestal and into it the food container in turn hangs. The next logical development (especially in France) was to substitute for the food bowl a covered cup with an elongated bottom that fits into the *bain-marie* and that could be used directly without the need of pouring; this was especially suitable for warm milk.

Near the beginning of the nineteenth century the European potters merged the tea kettle with the food warmer to produce the type of veilleuse that became most popular and that is most frequently seen in shops and in private collections today (although very few are displayed in museums), i.e., the pedestal with a teapot on the top. Only very rarely was a teapot type made before 1800 (the principal exception, rather understandably, being Wedgwood), and, conversely, few food warmers were made after that date (again the exceptions were usually English).

The pedestal of the teapot veilleuse is usually circular, although some are oval or square, occasionally rectangular, hexagonal, octagonal, or (rarely) triangular. It generally is of smaller diameter than the pedestal of a food warmer, obviously due to the use of a smaller pot and the need for less heat. There are two types of tea warmer pedestal: most stand directly on the table and have an aperture for the *godet* similar to food warmers; the others rest on a separate base (the rim of which is usually about one inch high) and must be lifted so that the *godet* can be placed within the pedestal. The latter type, having no aperture, has, in order to permit a current of air, several small holes in the base and near the top of the pedestal. Toward the center of the base there is often a small circular ridge or a depression to hold the *godet* in proper position. The teapot itself is generally of conforming shape, design, and decoration, but often the pot is merely gilded, especially when the pedestal is decorated with an encircling painted scene or with scenic panels.

The teapot veilleuses were made in many shapes. Some have a pedestal in the form of a circular tower with a crenelated upper rim; these rest on a separate base and the decoration is often an encircling landscape or a panel showing a well-known city square or a scene from some opera. A rather similar type, but usually of porcelain less fine and translucent, substitutes for the crenelation a beaded edge.

Some veilleuses have the pedestal made of lithophane (Berlin transparency), and are rectangular with four panels or triangular with three panels, or occasionally circular. These are especially effective when illuminated and the decorative scene or design appears as though it were grisaille. (See Chapter 4.)

A wholly different type of veilleuse was developed in France about 1830, as mentioned above, and is generally associated with the name of Jacob Petit. (See Chapter 4.) These are known as *personnages*.[3] They are ornately modeled and colorfully decorated figures representing a wide variety of characters. One hundred and one different models (practically all of which are of French origin) are known, and in addition many of

these were made with variations of modeling detail (see Figs. P–24 and P–25) or of color. The models were molded for reproduction and the number of each that was cast is unknown; but the ones in the form of two marquises of the French court (Figs. P–2 and P–3), a monk (Fig. P–43), and a nun (Fig. P–44) were, judging from known specimens extant today, among the most popular, followed by a young Bacchus riding a goat (Fig. P–74).

The *personnages* are usually divided midway into two parts. The bottom half is the usual hollow pedestal, with an aperture in the rear to insert the *godet* or with a separate base for the pedestal and the *godet* to stand on. The upper half is the teapot, generally modeled so that an upraised arm of the figure is the spout, the other arm the handle. Sometimes the spout is in the headdress, and occasionally there is a small handle attached at the rear. The lid is frequently an ornamental hat or headdress (often missing today).

As a departure from *personnages*, but almost as ornate, there are the veilleuses of architectural design, some of which were also made by Jacob Petit. Among these are pieces suggestive of cathedrals (round, rectangular, hexagonal, or octagonal) with rose windows or stained-glass Gothic windows, as well as some in the form of various edifices. (See Chapter 4.)

Some veilleuses were made of wood, particularly "in countries where there was a predominantly peasant population, living in scattered communities. It was obviously a very unsuitable material, as is shown by the charred under-surface of the top rims of those that have survived. Although, in all probability, wooden specimens were very common on account of their cheapness, very few have survived for the reason above given, and they are now a great rarity."[4] An English collector of such wooden veilleuses who reports having seen them in Scandinavia and Holland has a Norwegian one of oak, rectangular in shape and with the carved date 1761, and an English one, oval in shape, made of mahogany with reeded sides and a brass lining.[5] These two, together with another in mahogany, square and eighteenth-century English, are in the Pinto Collection of Wooden Bygones, Birmingham Museum and Art Gallery, England.

A silver veilleuse, in the Nan Kivell Collection at the National Library of Australia, Canberra, is a counter-

23

part of the conventional Wedgwood tea warmer shown in Fig. 7. It was made by Rebecca Emes and Edward Barnard and bears on the cover an interesting engraved inscription: "This most gracious improvement of a comfort indispensably necessary in a sick chamber was most graciously presented to Sir Joseph Banks by the Queen, when Her Majesty, accompanied by her daughters their Royal Highnesses the Princesses Augusta and Mary honoured his family with a visit to Spring Grove on Monday October 4th 1813." Engraved on the pedestal is Queen Charlotte's cipher and crown.[6] The piece includes a silver burner (lamp) with a wick rising through a hole in its circular cover. Another similar silver veilleuse, made by James Emes in 1807 (but whose lamp was made in 1812), also bears an engraved royal cipher and crown, as well as the initial "M."[7]

In fairly early days in the United States replicas of ceramic veilleuses, both food warmers and tea warmers, were made of tole ware or japanned tin. (See Chapter 17). And from the Far East come metal veilleuses in conventional tea warmer shape, but having a flat-bottom pot. Japan has produced such pieces made of chased brass, probably in the late nineteenth century.[8] A bronze tea warmer of unknown (probably Asiatic) origin has ornate relief decoration, including a group of primitively modeled animals encircling the pedestal; examples are in the Berthelot and Freed Collections. Another bronze veilleuse, in a French collection, has a cylindrical pedestal, with one large loop handle, resting on a square base with four feet and pierced rim, and its conventional teapot has an overhead loop handle; the entire piece is of *bronze doré*.

To complete the picture, there are miniature ceramic tea warmers. Some, about 7 inches high, are usable, but others, only 5 inches high, are obviously for amusement only. There are also some rare samples or toys, about 2 to 4 inches high, made in France and England (Bloor Derby) in the middle of the nineteenth century; these are not to be confused with the many souvenir miniature veilleuses being made in France today. A collection of miniature veilleuses is owned by Mr. Theodore R. Jarvis, New York City; and there are eight miniatures in the Newman Collection, as well as one of lusterware at the Art Institute of Chicago.

Reproductions of the nineteenth-century tea warmers and cup warmers, as well as veilleuses of contemporary design, are being made today in France, Italy, Portugal, and Japan. These may appeal to decorators but have no interest for collectors. (See Chapter 19).

The largest known collection of veilleuses has been assembled by Dr. Frederick C. Freed of New York City, who since 1929 has accumulated over 650, of which he has donated 525 to his home town of Trenton, Tennessee, which exhibits them in its Municipal Building; all of the Freed Collection are of the nineteenth-century teapot type, including 66 different models of *personnages* and some unusual specimens of teapot veilleuses, but practically all are French (including over 50 conventionally shaped pieces made or decorated in comparatively recent years).[9] An outstanding collection belongs to Nobile Dott. Mario Chiavassa of Milan, Italy, who has over 500 pieces (including many duplicate models), almost all French or Italian tea warmers, of which about 150 are *personnages* (about 60 different models). The important collection of Sig. Valentino Brosio of Rome, Italy, 226 tea warmers (mostly French, a few Italian), was acquired in 1960 by the Museo Civico (Palazzo Madama), Turin, Italy. Other major collections, consisting principally of French nineteenth-century tea warmers, are the Berthelot Collection (about 500), Paris, France, the Broulard Collection (about 250) at Baumes-les-Messieurs, Jura, France, the Gandur Collection (about 170) at Orléans, France, and the Kraft Collection (about 100) at Geneva, Switzerland.[10] The largest group of food warmers (40 English specimens) is in the Pediatric Collection of the late Dr. T. G. H. Drake, at the Academy of Medicine, Toronto, Canada. Another large group of English food warmers (about 30) is at the Wellcome Historical Medical Museum, London. The Newman Collection (about 135), of Metairie, Louisiana (but now in London), includes many eighteenth-century food warmers and has examples from all the European countries (except Holland and Spain) that produced veilleuses.

The term *veilleuse* will be restricted here to apply to utensils for bedside use by one person. Excluded, therefore, although they are functionally very closely related, are large flat-bottom pottery and porcelain kettles resting on a ceramic stand containing a burner; these are generally similar in form to the usual silver kettle on a brazier. For the same reason, also excluded here are certain coffee-making pots on a pedestal containing a *godet*, as well as tall, thin porcelain warming urns in the form of a hollow column with a spigot, which provide for heating the liquid in the column by means of a *godet* inserted in an aperture in the plinth. Some specimens of these kettles, coffee-makers, and urns are described in Chapter 17.

# 2. Precursors of the Ceramic Veilleuse

The earliest known ceramic object in the form of a food warmer veilleuse that provided for heating food is from a tomb in Olbia, on the Black Sea in southern Russia, made in the Greco-Roman period about the first century B.C., and now in the British Museum.[11] This terra cotta piece is in the form of a circular shrine resting on a square plinth and divided into an upper and a lower chamber by means of a floor pierced with holes. The upper part is adorned with four fluted half-columns and has slits as air vents. There is an aperture in the front of the upper and lower chambers to insert whatever was the source of heat, possibly a lamp but more likely charcoal. A circular food bowl is suspended entirely within the upper part (anticipating the Sèvres tea warmer shown in Fig. 22) and has two small erect loop handles to lift it out.

Another ancestor is a curious Spanish piece of Manises pottery from the second half of the fifteenth century.[12] The pedestal is a small white pottery charcoal burner, and atop it rests a round flat-bottom white pottery bowl with a cover. It has been in the collection of Manual González Martí.

Several bronze pieces of the late fifteenth or early sixteenth century, made in Venice, are in the form of the eighteenth-century ceramic food warmers and are remarkably similar in size, shape, proportion, and operation. They probably were used as perfume burners. Two specimens are in the Louvre, Paris.[13] They have cylindrical pedestals resting on three feet, with a warming bowl set entirely within the pedestal. The pedestal

has a small hinged door over the aperture for the *godet*. These pieces are of gilded bronze, with intricately wrought openwork and with embellishment of blue enamel. Three similar pieces (differing only in that the finial is flat instead of spiral) are in the Musée Jacquemart-André, Paris[14]; another (without finial) is in the Bargello, Florence,[15] and another is in the private collection of M. Nicolas Landau, Paris.

Although it might reasonably be expected that the precursor of the European ceramic tea warmer would come from the tea-loving Far East, there is only one known comparable piece from before 1750 that functions as a true veilleuse, i.e., whose source of heat is a flame. It is in the Warren Cox Collection, and the owner has described this Chinese specimen thus: "Unique teapot of Ch'u-chou *yao* (ware) made in four pieces, a lamp with support for a circular wick on saucer, a reticulated stand, the pot itself and a cover. A most ingenious device in the pot causes the tea to heat quicker. By means of a bent hollow cone the heat is conducted up through the center of the pot. Late Ming or K'ang Hsi period (1662-1722). I have never seen anything else like it."[16] In fact, this piece is very similar in appearance and operation (except that its teapot has a flat bottom) to the European tea warmers of a century later.

In the family tree of the veilleuse one line goes back to the simple oil night lamp. (See Chapter 17.) The other stems from the various ceramic articles designed to keep food warm not by a flame but by the use of hot water or hot sand. Of the latter group, there are several

26

interesting specimens from early China. Those in the form of warming plates or bowls were very similar in appearance to their modern counterparts. Some specimens of these will be discussed in Chapter 17.

A Chinese piece that in form closely resembles a tea-warmer veilleuse but does not derive its heat from a flame is in the Metropolitan Museum of Art, New York. It is described by Warren Cox as a "wine pot and jar of the Yung-chêng period (1723-35) and decorated with underglaze blue and red. The pieces are fitted nicely together to form what appears to be a gourd wine pot. It is thought that hot water was placed in the lower jar to keep the wine warm."[17] The jar has animal-head handles, similar to the European food warmers hereinafter described.

The Japanese tea ceremony equipment sometimes included a small pottery charcoal stove on which rested an iron kettle[18] or a two-tiered iron charcoal burner and kettle.

In France, c. 1678, there were made "*pots à preparer le thé*," which consisted of tall ceramic stands with four curved legs attached to a round base on which rested a lamp; atop the stand was a flat-bottom teapot.[19] An example is the Berthelot Collection.

More closely related, especially to the tea-warmer veilleuses, are the large flat-bottom kettles that rest on a stand containing a heating device and that were made from about 1745 in England, Holland, France, Germany, and Switzerland. These are described in Chapter 17.

# 3. England

English potters in many regions of the country made ceramic food warmers for pap and gruel from about 1750 until more than a hundred years later. Most of them were of glazed earthenware (principally Bristol or Lambeth delft, Whieldon, Wedgwood, Leeds, and Staffordshire) but a few were made of porcelain (Chelsea and Lowestoft) and some of stoneware. England, although today thought of as a nation of tea drinkers, produced few tea warmers in the eighteenth century, as tea was then a costly luxury and its users did not relish it unless freshly brewed; but a few English glazed earthenware (Wedgwood) and porcelain tea warmers are known to have been made, mostly in the early nineteenth century.

English delftware food warmers, c. 1750-55, are among the earliest ceramic veilleuses. A typical one of Lambeth delft (Fig. 1) and another of Bristol delft (incomplete) are in the Apothecary Shop at Colonial Williamsburg, Virginia. Another, of Bristol delft, c. 1750, in the Victoria and Albert Museum, London, is complete with covered bowl and matching *godet*.[20] These pieces (those from Bristol and from Lambeth being almost indistinguishable, even by experts) are of tin-glazed pale blue earthenware, and the decoration is a painted cobalt blue floral and lattice design. Above the aperture and on the reverse, male masks in bold relief conceal air vents. The shallow globular-shaped bowl has a rim rising about 1 inch above the flange and has two upslanting acanthus-leaf handles; its underside is unglazed. The cover of the bowl is surmounted (as was frequent with early English food warmers) by a candle holder; this indicates the evolution of the veilleuse from the simple night lamp. The special features of this type of pedestal have been described thus: "Two substantial solid scrolls placed about half-way up the pedestal serve as handles, with three projecting lugs below, finger-width apart, enabling the piece to be grasped securely . . . One may note the wreathing visible on the inner wall of the pedestal. This slight unevenness of surface was used to strengthen the body, which softened at one period during firing and tended to collapse beneath the weight. The slight variation in thickness provided by wreathing was sufficient to prevent this."[21] A more likely explanation is that the wreathing is the mark of the potter's fingers as the piece turned on the wheel, especially as earthenware was not heated to a point of vitrification such as might cause porcelain to collapse; and it is pertinent to note that porcelain, which might collapse, rarely shows such wreathing.

A similar delftware food warmer, said by W. J. Pountney to have been produced by Joseph Flower at Bristol and at one time to have been in the private collection of Flower's great-granddaughter, Mrs. E. J. Swann, of Bristol, has been described as a "caudle cup or pap warmer . . . showing the Eastern style of decoration, with the lattice bands on all three sections of it . . . Flower seems to have produced a great number of these beautiful little pieces."[22] As Flower made pottery only from

28

Fig. 1. Lambeth delft tin-glazed earthenware, c. 1750-55.
Colonial Williamsburg Collection, Williamsburg, Virginia.

1743,[23] these pieces must date from after that year except for the doubt that has been cast on the assumption that Flower in fact made these family-inherited pieces attributed to him.[24] In any event, no food warmer of any English delftware pottery, or any other English pottery, has been established as having been made before 1750.[25]

Similarly modeled English delftware food warmers are not uncommon. On some the mask is more pronounced and more sharply modeled. The hand-painted decoration varies on each piece, with different lattice-work, floral sprays, and bands. The Henry Francis du Pont Winterthur Museum, Winterthur, Delaware, has two complete pieces and two without the bowl and cover. One of Bristol delft, complete, is in the Wellcome Historical Medical Museum, London.[26] Another, of Bristol delft, complete, in the delftware collection of Dr. Warren Baker, Michigan City, Indiana, has been exhibited at the Chicago Art Institute,[27] and there is a second such piece in the Baker Collection. A like piece, of Bristol delft, complete with bowl, cover, and *godet*, in the Newman Collection, was acquired at the 1965 sale of the delftware collection of the late Professor F. H. Garner, and several other such pieces (some incomplete) were sold in its wake at 1965 London sales.[28] A complete example is in the delftware collection of Mr. Louis L. Lipski, London. Three such food warmers, incomplete, attributed to Bristol are in the City Museum, Stoke-on-Trent, England. The Drake Pediatric Collection, at the Academy of Medicine, Toronto, Canada, has eight delftware food warmers of this type (four of which are merely pedestals).[29] A similar pedestal is in the Royal Scottish Museum, Edinburgh, and another is in the collection of the Pharmaceutical Society of Great Britain, London. A like delftware food warmer, in the Broulard Collection, differs from all the others in that the cover has, instead of a candleholder, a solid scroll finial similar to the scroll handles on the pedestal. Two other delftware pedestals were offered for sale in 1962 by a dealer near Boston, Massachusetts.

A cylindrical glazed earthenware pedestal, similar in shape, size, and modeling to the above-described delftware pedestals with male masks, solid scroll handles, and holding lugs, but quite differently decorated, is in the Drake Collection. (Fig. 2.) Its decoration substitutes a floral pattern without lattices or other formal motifs.

Fig. 2. English (western) delft, c. 1750-60. Drake Collection, Academy of Medicine, Toronto, Canada.

The underglaze blue of the flowers has run into the white ground, giving an overall bluish tinge. There is an underglaze numeral 5 on the base. The masks, albeit thinner, have the same sharp chins, flat noses, and pronounced features as the above-described delftware pedestals, and the piece has the Chinese style of decoration that often was used on delftware in the eighteenth century. Considering the body, modeling, and decoration, the piece is almost certainly English delft even though it is the only known delftware pedestal so decorated.

Quite different in form is a Lambeth delft food warmer in the Wellcome Museum. (Fig. 3.) Instead of being severely cylindrical like the usual delft pedestals, this one is baluster-shaped with two uplifted shell-like handles. The shape and modeling, similar to that of the Staffordshire food warmer at Leeuwarden (Fig. 18) and

Fig. 3. Lambeth delft, c. 1750-55. Wellcome Historical
Medical Museum, London.

Fig. 4. Lowestoft, 1770-75. Norwich Castle Museum, Norwich, England.

32

the Ginori (Doccia) piece in Rome (Fig. 92), suggests a common ancestor in silver, and perhaps also an itinerant modeler. The white body of this Lambeth delft food warmer, especially of the bowl and cover, has a pinkish cast, with the underglaze decoration in dark blue. The bowl has flat protruding handles and its cover has a socket for a candle.

A glazed earthenware food warmer pedestal, slightly conical instead of cylindrical, in the Drake Collection, has been attributed to delftware from western England. It has two dog's-head masks as handles and two hooded air vents in the form of the Continental food warmer pedestals hereinafter discussed. The piece is decorated overall in powder puce, with six reserved cartouches of floral sprays in green, red, and yellow.

Lowestoft porcelain food warmers were also made in the middle of the eighteenth century. One, bearing on its base the painter's numeral 5 and therefore probably not later than 1775, is in the Castle Museum, Norwich, England. (Fig. 4.) In form and decoration it is somewhat like the usual delftware food warmers. The cylindrical pedestal has two satan-like masks (one over the aperture and the other on the reverse) and two shell-shaped hoods over the vents; the bowl has two uplifted handles, and the low-domed cover has a candle socket. It is decorated with floral sprays in underglaze blue.

A similar Lowestoft food warmer, also with the numeral 5, has been sold three times at Sotheby's, London, in 1938 (from the Wallace Elliot Collection), in 1955 (from the Hotblack Collection), and in 1959 (from the Geoffrey Godden Collection), having once been exhibited at Christchurch Mansion Museum, Ipswich.[30] The 1955 Sotheby Catalogue described it as "an unusually fine example of this rare type of object which has counterparts in Continental porcelain and in English delft and Whieldon lead glazed wares." Another similar Lowestoft food warmer was also sold at Sotheby's in 1961 (from the D. M. Hunting Collection); the catalogue described it as "a fine Lowestoft 'Pap' Warmer of typical cylindrical form, in three sections complete with lamp and wick trailer, boldly decorated with sprays of flowers and butterflies and moulded with double ear and shell handles with two superbly modelled mitered heads, the cover surmounted by a candle nozzle, 10 in., rare painter's numeral 5,55, triangle and arrow and annulet in

underglaze-blue. Perhaps one of the most complete examples yet recorded."[31] Two other Lowestoft food warmer pedestals are in the Drake Collection; they are similarly modeled but have slightly different floral decoration. The pedestal of another such piece is in the Lowestoft Collection of Mr. G. W. Middleton, of Lowestoft, England.

A somewhat different Lowestoft food warmer pedestal, c. 1765-70, is in the Castle Museum, Norwich, having been acquired at the 1962 sale of the Hunting Collection.[32] Although of the same shape as the others already described and with the same shell hoods and painter's numeral 5, its unique masks are different, depicting in bold relief a male head of Oriental mien. The decoration is underglaze blue with flower sprays and insects. The accompanying cover, probably c. 1775-90 and not originally for this piece, has a finial in the form of the head of a *putto* identical with the heads of two *putto* figurines made at Lowestoft.[33]

Probably the rarest English food warmer is a porcelain one in the Drake Collection, Toronto; it is from Chelsea, c. 1758, and bears the red anchor mark.[34] (Plate II.) Its tall, thin pedestal, in cylindrical form, has a sun-god mask over the aperture and two foliated double scroll handles. The warming bowl, also higher than the usual bowls, has two uplifted scroll handles, and its cover is surmounted by a candle socket with encircling pierced slits. The decoration is polychrome enamel floral sprays and gilt.

A Whieldon food warmer of tortoise-shell-glazed earthenware, c. 1760, probably by Ralph Wood, is in the collection of Colonial Williamsburg. (Fig. 5.) The cylindrical pedestal, slightly wider than those of delftware and Lowestoft, has two foliated loop handles and, above the very wide aperture, a female-head mask with long braids; small holes beside the nostrils serve as air vents in addition to several holes in diamond-shaped groups of four. The bowl has two angular loop crabstock handles, and its cover has a flat flower finial. The whole piece is glazed with mottled hues of gray and green. A similar complete Whieldon piece is in the Burnap Collection at the Nelson Gallery and Atkins Museum, Kansas City, Missouri.[35] Another such Whieldon piece, complete, was sold in 1938 from the Wallace Elliot Collection,[36] and two additional food warmers of

Fig. 5. Whieldon tortoise-shell glazed earthenware, c. 1760.
Colonial Williamsburg Collection, Williamsburg, Virginia.

34

Plate I. Sèvres, *pâte tendre coquetière,* 1759. Rothschild
Collection, Waddesdon Manor, Aylesbury, England.

Plate II. Chelsea, red anchor mark, c. 1758. Dr. T. G. H.
Drake Collection, Academy of Medicine, Toronto, Canada.

Plate III. Sèvres, *pâte tendre*, c. 1770-71. Newman Collection.

Plate IV. France. Jacob Petit, c. 1830. Newman Collection.

Plate V. France. *Personnage*, Madame Du Barry, 1830-50. Broulard Collection, Baumes-les-Messieurs, France.

Plate VII. France. *Personnage,* musketeer, 1830-50. Broulard Collection, Baumes-les-Messieurs, France.

Plate VI. Bohemia. *Personnages,* Chinese mandarin and mandariness, Schlaggenwald, c. 1840. Georges Berthelot Collection, Paris.

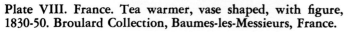
Plate VIII. France. Tea warmer, vase shaped, with figure, 1830-50. Broulard Collection, Baumes-les-Messieurs, France.

Plate IX. France. *Personnage,* grotesque human, 1830-50. Collection of Mme. Raoul Kraft, Geneva.

Plate X. France. *Personnage,* Amphitrite riding dolphin. Jacob Petit, 1830-50. Newman Collection.

Plate XI. France. Tea warmer, triangular, 1830-50. Broulard Collection, Baumes-les-Messieurs, France.

Plate XII. France. Tea warmer, Persian temple, c. 1814-30. Newman Collection.

**Plate XIII.** Nymphenburg. Johann Häringer, 1763. Stadtarchiv, Rosenheim, Germany.

Plate XIV. Gorbunovo (Moscow). A. Popoff, 1830-40.
Newman Collection.

Plate XV. Lenzburg, Switzerland. Johann Jacob Frey, c.
1765. Newman Collection.

Plate XVI. Vista Alegre, Portugal. Victor François Chartier Rousseau, c. 1835. Pinto-Basto Collection, Ilhova, Portugal.

this type were offered for sale in New York City in 1964.[37]

There are two other Whieldon food warmers in the Drake Collection. One is very similar to those described above in its general form, but its pedestal has no masks, its bowl has two flat shell-shaped handles, and its cover has a tall candle socket; it is glazed gray, mottled with pale yellow, red, and green. The other, somewhat bulbous, has a pedestal with interlaced loop handles and no masks, and its lipped bowl has one small loop handle; there are floral appliqués around the aperture and at the handle terminals, and the glaze is puce colored.[38]

Wedgwood made a large number of food warmers and also tea warmers of cream-colored glazed earthenware, the famed and popular Queen's Ware. The *Queen's Ware Catalogue, 1774*, refers to "Night Lamps, to keep any Liquid warm all night," and examples are known dated 1871, so that "these heaters were made in cream ware for at least one hundred years. Around the middle of the nineteenth century, they were very popular as may be seen by the number mentioned in the catalogue of the Great Exhibition of 1851."[39]

The Wedgwood pieces vary from 9 to 12 inches in height (to the top of the finial), and early nineteenth-century priced catalogues quoted varying prices for four different sizes of both the food warmer and the tea warmer (as well as alternative prices for "best" and "second" qualities in creamware and in printed ware). The pedestal, for interchangeable use with a warming bowl (and liner) and a teapot, usually has two large plain loop handles and a pierced "leafage" floral spray over the aperture (none on the reverse); on the inside there is a circular ridge to hold the *godet* in center position. The *godet* itself (now seldom found) was usually a simple semi-globular cup, with a small loop handle, for oil and wick, but some had a lid with a center hole for a wick and other holes as air vents; and the catalogue design for one heating device (no example is known) was rather intricate, with a long-handled tripod (to hold the wick) set in the "lamp-cup."[40] The warming bowl conforms to the cylindrical shape of the pedestal and usually has two interlaced strap handles, a pouring lip, and a cover with an acorn or a knob finial. The teapot of the typical Wedgwood tea warmer is modeled to carry upward the lines of the pedestal and usually has a three-sectioned loop handle over the top; it has a protruding globular bottom that fits well into the pedestal. The food warmer often has a separate cylindrical liner (as did many of the Leeds and Staffordshire pieces), at least after 1817.[41]

The 1774 *Wedgwood Queen's Ware Catalogue*,[42] the earliest such catalogue,[43] shows the design for a cream-ware tea warmer which is the earliest known depiction of or reference to a veilleuse with a teapot. The 1817 *Wedgwood Queen's Ware Catalogue*[44] shows the design of the characteristic Wedgwood pedestal with a food warmer bowl[45] and a teapot for interchangeable use. The 1817 Catalogue design has the pierced leafage spray that appears on all known Wedgwood food warmers and tea warmers. The 1774 Catalogue design shows a pedestal with somewhat different pierced work and a teapot with a wide flange more like the tea warmer shown in Fig. 16 (and those from Treviso, Italy) than the later Wedgwood streamlined tea warmers; no example of this 1774 design has been located.

One typical Wedgwood Queen's Ware food warmer, dated 1871 but similar to earlier ones, privately owned, has been described as a "Night-lamp with covered pap-warmer and inner pan for water."[46] (The "inner pan" was the liner.) There are two similar marked pieces in the Historisches Museum, Basel, Switzerland; one, 1872, in the City Museum and Art Gallery, Stoke-on-Trent, England; one in the Buten Museum, Merion, Pennsylvania[47] (Fig. 6); three (of which two are pedestals only) in the Drake Collection; one in the Chiavassa Collection; and one in the Newman Collection. Two other cream-ware food warmers, unmarked and so perhaps not Wedgwood, in the Wellcome Museum, have pedestals and bowls conforming to the usual Wedgwood shape and decoration, and there are also three signed Wedgwood bowls and liners without the pedestal.

A typical Wedgwood tea warmer, marked "Etruria," early nineteenth century, is in the J. L. Dixon Collection at the Victoria and Albert Museum.[48] (Fig. 7.) There are two at the Wellcome Museum, one slightly larger than the other. Other Wedgwood creamware tea warmers in this same form are in the Wedgwood Museum, Barlaston, England,[49] and the Rijksmuseum Twenthe, Enschede, Holland, and one was in the Historical Museum, Frankfurt, Germany, before its destruction in World War II.[50] Another, c. 1850, is in the Buten Mu-

Fig. 6. Wedgwood. Buten Museum of Wedgwood, Merion, Pennsylvania.

Fig. 7. Wedgwood (Etruria), early nineteenth century.
Victoria and Albert Museum, London.

Fig. 8. Wedgwood. Collection of Miss Elaine Denby, London.

seum, and there are specimens in the Chiavassa and Drake Collections, and also in the Newman Collection.[51] One, similar but unmarked, possibly not Wedgwood, is in the Princessehof Museum, Leeuwarden, Holland.

Another such Wedgwood tea warmer, in the collection of Mrs. Nina Fletcher Little, Brookline, Massachusetts, has been described as "A Queen's ware kettle and stand for a sick-room or nursery which without a doubt was the eighteenth century prototype of Howe's patented nursery lamp of the nineteenth century."[52] This piece differs from the other Wedgwood tea warmers in that its cover (perhaps not the original) has pierced slits to serve as vents for escaping steam.

A few Wedgwood veilleuses vary from the conventional form. A early food warmer, c. 1780-90, in the collection of Miss Elaine Denby, London, is the only known Wedgwood veilleuse that has, instead of single loop handles on the pedestal, interlaced strap loop handles, the terminals of which (characteristic of Wedgwood handles in general) curl outward from the pedestal; the bowl has the usual interlaced strap handles and the cover has an artichoke finial. (Fig. 8.) In addition to the two conventionally modeled Wedgwood tea warmers in the Wellcome Museum, one slightly larger than usual, the other somewhat smaller, an early marked piece of the smaller size is owned by Sir Ralph and Lady Richardson, London.

Four veilleuses of unconventional form are illustrated in the *Wedgwood First Shape Book*.[53] One has a low pedestal (about 3 inches high) but with characteristic Wedgwood aperture and pierced work, a shallow bowl that fits completely within the pedestal, and a cover with a ring finial.[54] Another also has a low pedestal in which rests a liner and a very tall cylindrical bowl; a curious elongated spout projects from the liner apparently to permit steam to escape so as to avoid vibrating the pot.[55] The third is like the typical food warmers except that the finial is shaped like a thistle[56]; such a piece is in the Buten Museum of Wedgwood. The fourth is like the usual tea warmers except that the pedestal has solid scroll handles (instead of loops) and the pot has a shield above the spout, as many Wedgwood teapots do.[57]

All the Wedgwood pieces heretofore mentioned are of undecorated cream-colored Queen's Ware. Some Wedgwood creamware food warmers and tea warmers of con-

ventional shape were transfer-printed in blue with encircling rural landscapes. There is one such food warmer in the Drake Collection, another in the Chiavassa Collection, and one (with a conforming blue *godet*) in the Brosio Collection.[58] In the Newman Collection there is such a food warmer, marked Wedgwood and dated "AYS," with the unusual decoration of sprays, apparently of seaweed, printed in brown. A Wedgwood tea warmer, marked but without date letters, in the Newman Collection, is decorated with ornate floral sprays printed in blue.

Wedgwood also made food warmers and tea warmers of pearlware which have a faint bluish tinge, especially in the grooves where the coloring accumulated. One such tea warmer, in the collection of Mr. Byron A. Born, New York City, is in the traditional shape with the usual leafage pierced spray, but it also has a linear decoration painted in blue encircling the pedestal and the pot, as well as along the sides of the handles of the pedestal and the pot.[59] A pearlware food warmer, with the impressed date mark "ONV" and complete with liner, bowl, and cover, is in the Newman Collection; its height is only 9 inches.

There is a tendency to attribute to Wedgwood various Continental creamware veilleuses that are not remotely in the style of Wedgwood, as will be indicated later. This is apart from the contemporaneous pieces made in Germany, Switzerland, and Italy by potters who frankly imitated Wedgwood creamware in form and decoration.

A food warmer of unglazed red stoneware with rose-engine-turned wavy decoration is in the Colonial Williamsburg Collection. (Fig. 9.) The cylindrical pedestal and covered lipped bowl, while basically similar to the Wedgwood and particularly the Whieldon food warmers, have marked differences. All three sections have gadroon rims, and the aperture of the pedestal is differently shaped. The pedestal has foliated loop handles attached by unusual projecting lugs, and the bowl has rustic loop handles. There is no mask, and the only pierced work is four clusters of four small holes in diamond formation, as on the Whieldon pedestals. The pedestal and the bowl bear pseudo-Chinese seal marks, and on the *godet* there is an oval mark including the letter "P."[60] Although Josiah Wedgwood made rose-engine-turned redware in 1765, after acquiring his first engine-turning lathe in 1763 from Boulton and Fothergill, a metal-turning fac-

Fig. 9. Red stoneware rose-engine-turned food warmer, pseudo-Chinese marks, c. 1760. Colonial Williamsburg Collection, Williamsburg, Virginia.

tory in Birmingham,[61] the attribution to him (as against other English potters making like wares even earlier) of any such engine-turned pieces with pseudo-Chinese seal marks has been seriously questioned.[62] Despite the overall shape of the piece, attribution to Wedgwood or Whieldon is not warranted in view of the aperture shape, the gadroon rims, and the handles, all unlike any other food warmer from these sources. Rose-engine-turned red stoneware with pseudo-Chinese marks was also made at Leeds, c. 1770[63] (and the red stoneware rose-engine-turned kettle mentioned in Chapter 17, modeled and decorated very similarly to the Leeds creamware kettles there also mentioned, has recently been attributed to Leeds); but, although gadroon rims are on one food warmer attributed to Leeds, they and the handles here are not characteristic of that factory and raise some doubt. The Sotheby Catalogue for the 1958 sale of this piece[64] suggested that it was "perhaps Astbury," the Staffordshire potter who worked an engine lathe for the Elers,[65] and a reference was made to similar-type red engine-turned wares in the Dr. J. W. L. Glaisher Collection, one jug with a gadroon foot rim and a square Chinese seal mark and another jug marked "Astbury"[66]; but John Astbury died in 1743, which would preclude him as the maker of a piece in this form, although perhaps not his son Thomas. Another possibility, suggested by the letter "P" on the *godet*, is Humphrey Palmer, a Staffordshire potter who made rose-engine-turned ware, 1760-78, in imitation of Wedgwood.[67] Considering all the factors, the provenance of this piece cannot be established at this time.

A curious spherical food-warmer pedestal with one loop handle is in the Drake Collection.[68] (Fig. 10.) It is of red clay body and light brown glaze, decorated with tulips and roses in green and yellow slip. The square aperture for the *godet* is fitted with a square door-like cover; slits in this cover and in the pedestal enable the cover to be tied closed. It is marked in slip "16 Dec. 1751" with the initials "IH". Its provenance has not been determined, but it may be from Staffordshire or possibly from a pottery in Sussex.

Leeds produced, in the second half of the eighteenth century, a number of cream-colored glazed earthenware food warmers, all of a deeper hue than the Wedgwood pieces. These varied considerably in form and decora-

tion, unlike those from other English potteries which tended to produce one basic model. But one Leeds model that was occasionally repeated has a pedestal that is somewhat baluster-shaped (bowed and slightly waisted), rather than the usual cylindrical shape. Its feature is two relief masks, over the aperture and on the reverse, of a woman's head with long hanging braids (similar to the masks on the Whieldon food warmers described above and shown in Fig. 5). The pedestal has two double interlaced reeded loop handles attached by floral terminals, and the decoration is four pierced designs and a relief floral pattern bordering the aperture. The bowl is suspended by a flanged edge within a liner and has usually two side handles. The cover of the bowl has a relief floral spray, a projecting lid over the lip of the bowl, and a tall candle socket having a pierced slit (to facilitate removing the candle stub).

A complete Leeds creamware food warmer of the type described, c. 1775, is in the collection of Mr. Donald C. Towner, London; its bowl has only one loop handle which is of an unusual shape.[69] (Fig. 11.) Another similar piece (but lacking the bowl) is in the Victoria and Albert Museum.[70] Two similar Leeds food warmers are in the Drake Collection; one is identical except for more elaborate floral terminals on the pedestal, and the other has slightly different pierced-work patterns. Another such pedestal, substantially similar, is in the Wellcome Museum, which also has a pedestal of similar ware and form but without masks and with identical loop handles, perhaps Leeds of a later period. A complete creamware food warmer of the same shape, in the Newman Collection, is perhaps not Leeds; its pedestal has single loop handles and different female masks (with a draped headdress instead of the braids) and is without any relief floral decoration.

Other Leeds creamware food warmers are each of unique form, only one example of each model being known. The Drake Collection has one with a baluster-shaped pedestal similar to those described above, with the same handles and floral terminals, but instead of any masks it has an encircling pattern of vertical reeding and different pierced design; the cover of the bowl is similarly reeded and its finial is a seated figure (broken). (Fig. 12.) Another Leeds creamware pedestal in the Drake Collection is cylindrically shaped, with interlaced reeded

Fig. 10. Brown-glazed red clay with slip decoration, 1751.
Drake Collection, Academy of Medicine, Toronto.

loop handles attached by the usual floral terminals and with masks of bearded male heads; encircling the pedestal is a checkered pattern of vertical reeding. (Fig. 13.) Still another Leeds creamware food warmer, complete, in the Newman Collection, has a cylindrically shaped pedestal with interlaced loop strap handles and with two well-modeled masks in the form of ram's heads; the cover of the bowl has much pierced work and a flower finial. (Fig. 14.) In the Musée des Arts Décoratifs, Paris, there is a creamware food warmer attributed to Leeds that is very similar to the Wedgwood food warmers; its cylindrical pedestal has indented-loop strap handles, its bowl has two small loop handles, and the only decoration is a small gadroon rim on the pedestal and on the bowl.

Sometimes the lipped warming bowl of a Leeds food warmer, with a socket on the cover, has (instead of the usual two side handles) one small loop handle (opposite the lip) to facilitate pouring. This type has in one recent instance been called a "toddy warmer" and the deep socket has been said to be for a "tobacco taper."[71] One such Leeds creamware piece, in the City Art Gallery, Leeds, has a cylindrical pedestal, single-loop strap handles, relief female-head masks (with shell-like headdresses) above the aperture and on the reverse, and pierced-work design; its bowl is fluted and has a pouring lip and a single loop handle, and its cover has a tall socket.[72] The reason for this special designation of such a piece is not apparent. An almost identical Leeds creamware piece is in the collection of Mrs. Nina Fletcher Little, Brookline, Massachusetts; its only difference is that the handle of the bowl is curled and fluted instead of being a single loop.[73] (Fig. 15.)

42

Fig. 11. Leeds cream-colored glazed earthenware, c. 1775.
Collection of Mr. Donald C. Towner, London.

Fig. 13. Leeds cream-colored glazed earthenware, c. 1775.
Drake Collection, Academy of Medicine, Toronto.

Fig. 12. Leeds cream-colored glazed earthenware, c. 1775.
Drake Collection, Academy of Medicine, Toronto.

44

Fig. 14. Leeds cream-colored glazed earthenware, c. 1775. Newman Collection.

Fig. 15. Leeds cream-colored glazed earthenware, c. 1775. Mrs. Nina Fletcher Little Collection, Brookline, Massachusetts.

The only known tea warmer attributed to Leeds is a creamware piece in the City Art Gallery, Leeds. (Fig. 16.) It has a cylindrically shaped pedestal that is decorated with four low-relief lion's-head masks that are connected by double floral swags in relief and also with five encircling beaded bands and small groups of pierced work. The low pot is suspended by a wide flange and has a unique snip spout and a small loop handle. The masks and swags in this form are not known on other Leeds ware and should be compared with those on the pedestal of Italian attribution shown in Fig. 107. The whole piece has much in common with the creamware veilleuses from Treviso, Italy (such as the one shown in Fig. 103), especially the low pot, the wide flange, and the beaded bands. The possibility of Italian origin cannot be excluded.

A creamware food warmer in the Wellcome Museum has a tall pedestal with two large foliated loop handles and a wide aperture. (Fig. 17.) Its decoration, front and reverse, is sun-god masks, but quite differently modeled from the Chelsea masks shown in Plate II. The bowl has two conforming small loop handles and a cover with a candle socket. The provenance of this piece is uncertain.

Staffordshire creamware food warmers were made in various forms. Some were exported to Holland in the latter part of the eighteenth century and were advertised in newspapers of Leeuwarden, Holland. One such piece, in the Princessehof Museum, Leeuwarden, has a baluster pedestal decorated with elaborate relief floral garlands in the style often seen on silverware; it has scroll handles, shell-like hoods over the air vents (instead of masks), and a low candle holder on the cover. (Fig. 18.) It should be compared, as to shape and modeling, with the pieces shown in Fig. 3 and Fig. 92.

Undecorated food warmers, ranging in color from white to cream and with bodies varying from thin glazed earthenware to heavy stoneware or ironstone china were made in various English potteries in the late eighteenth and early nineteenth centuries. No salt-glazed example is known. Such pieces often came from Staffordshire but it is usually impossible to make definite attributions. These usually have cylindrical pedestals with two large loop handles (plain or foliated) and are undecorated except for pierced work in varying patterns that often

encircle the pedestal or at least the side with the aperture. Frequently the rim at the bottom of the aperture is higher than on other English pedestals. The bowls generally have two conforming small loop handles, a pouring lip, a liner, and a cover (flat or low-domed) with a ball, knob, or acorn finial. A typical piece is in the Drake Collection, except that its bowl has a single loop handle; its pierced work is in a lateral pattern. (Fig. 19.) This collection has two other such food warmers (one with a *godet*) whose pedestals are encircled with a pierced pattern of holes grouped in diamond form and whose bowls have two small loop handles and a flat cover with a ball finial; these are probably from Staffordshire, possibly Davenport or Spode, as is the blue transfer-printed piece in identical form described below. A complete such piece, with liner and *godet*, is in the pharmaceutical collection of Dr. Claude H. Spiers, London.

In this same group is a pedestal in the Colonial Williamsburg Collection that has foliated loop handles; with it is the original globular-shaped *godet* that has a center chimney for the wick. Two similar pedestals, with like foliated loop handles but whose pierced work is in a different pattern, are in the Wellcome Museum, one of which has a bowl with two loop handles, a liner, and a *godet* with a cover through which the wick passes.[74] In this same museum are also two other such food warmers except that they have plain loop handles and different pierced work. A comparable but undecorated food warmer is at the Boston Museum of Fine Arts (on loan).

Also in the Wellcome Museum are four white-glazed unmarked pieces that all have a characteristic tulip-shaped aperture. One has a cylindrical pedestal with loop handles and is complete with liner, bowl, and cover.[75] Another (lacking the cover), of identical modeling and pierced work, has an overall floral and butterfly decoration in underglaze blue transfer print.[76] The third is a similar white-glazed pedestal only. The fourth is complete and similar but slightly smaller.

A white-glazed food warmer pedestal, c. 1835, with the impressed mark "Davenport," in the Wellcome Museum, is cylindrically shaped, with large plain loop handles, a simple pointed aperture, and decoration of pierced holes that include four tiny hearts pointing toward a center hole; it has a floral pattern in underglaze blue. Two comparable, but unmarked, heavy white-

Fig. 16. Cream-colored glazed earthenware. Leeds City Art
Galleries, Leeds, England.

Fig. 17. Staffordshire creamware, 1770-90. Wellcome Historical Medical Museum, London.

Fig. 18. Staffordshire creamware, 1770-90. Princessehof Museum, Leeuwarden, Holland.

Fig. 19. English (probably Staffordshire) white-glazed pottery food warmer: bowl, pedestal, cover, liner. Drake Collection, Academy of Medicine, Toronto.

Fig. 20. English blue-transfer-printed. Mark: beehive and "Crystal Florentine China." Collection of Mrs. Nina Fletcher Little, Brookline, Massachusetts.

glazed food warmers include in their extensive pierced-work decoration on the pedestal, on the side of the aperture, four similarly arranged tiny heart-shaped holes and also have a simple pointed aperture, in both respects like the marked Davenport piece. But the large loop handles of the cylindrical pedestal are foliated rather than plain. One, complete with a lipped bowl, a cover with a candle socket, and a metal lamp (claimed to be the original), is in the Grace Lyman Stammers Collection, Bolton, Massachusetts.[77] The other, in the Newman Collection, has an identical pedestal but the cover of the bowl has a knob finial.

Creamware tea warmers, unlike food warmers, are usually identifiable as Wedgwood. But two unmarked such tea warmers, complete with liner, in the Wellcome Museum, while conforming in shape to the Wedgwood models, have features not known on other Wedgwood veilleuses. Each has tiny heart-shaped pierced work like the above-described Davenport food warmer and a tulip-shaped aperture. Their provenance, probably Staffordshire, has not now been established.

All the above-described white-glazed food warmers are undecorated except the one with the blue underglaze printed pattern. Some other white-glazed pieces of this type are also decorated in blue transfer. One, in the collection of Mrs. Nina Fletcher Little, has an overall transfer-printed blue floral and lattice pattern; it bears the mark of a beehive encircled by foliage and the words "Crystal Florentine China."[78] (Fig. 20.) It is probably a type of stoneware called in England "stone china," and the word "Florentine" probably refers to the type of decoration. The pedestal has plain loop handles and a pierced pattern, and the bowl (lacking the cover) has a pouring lip and a single loop handle; the globular *godet*, modeled exactly like the *godet* at Colonial Williamsburg, is similarly printed in blue. In the Newman Collection there is a heavy white-glazed food warmer, in the form of the Wedgwood food warmers, which is decorated with an overall blue transfer-printed floral pattern featuring a large planted urn entwined by a serpent; it is marked "Florentine Opaque China" and it also is of stoneware. Both of these pieces are probably from Staffordshire, c. 1840, possibly Davenport or Spode. A related piece, of like body, also in the Newman Collection, has a cylindrical pedestal (with unusual angular loop handles, a

tulip-shaped aperture, and an encircling pierced pattern), a completely recessed bowl (no handles), and a *godet*; all three sections are uniformly decorated with underglaze sponged blue on a white ground.

The pedestal of a food warmer marked "Spode" in blue script is said to be in an English private collection.[79] A food warmer whose cylindrical pedestal has foliated loop handles and is decorated with an encircling landscape printed in blue and with pierced work is in the Drake Collection; the cover (perhaps not the original) bears the circular mark "Copeland & Garret: late Spode." Another known food warmer marked "Copeland & Garret" has a cylindrical pedestal with foliated loop handles and a bowl with a small loop handle; it is white glazed without decoration.

The only known complete porcelain British tea warmer is one, in the Victoria and Albert Museum, that has often been attributed to Swansea, c. 1817.[80] (Fig. 21.) It has a circular tower pedestal with a crenelated upper rim, resting on a separate base, and its gilded teapot has an angular loop handle. The circular *godet* has a cover with a center chimney for the wick. The Museum's records attribute it to Swansea and state that the modeler was Isaac Wood and that the polychrome Italian landscape encircling the pedestal, with castle, bridges, and figures, was perhaps painted in London by Thomas Baxter. But the attribution to Swansea has recently been vehemently repudiated to this writer by Mr. W. J. Grant-Davidson, present Director of the Glynn Vivian Art Gallery at Swansea, and also by Mr. Geoffrey Godden, whose forthcoming book on early Minton porcelain will attribute this piece to Minton and will reproduce a drawing of an undecorated tea warmer of exactly the same form that appears as "No. 40 Night Lamp" in a *Minton Shape Book*, c. 1820-30, that is at the Minton factory. Although the piece resembles in basic form the many crenelated tower veilleuses from France and elsewhere, it has several modeling features that significantly are identical with the drawing, such as the unique angular loop handle with button terminal, the curved spout with relief molded design, the slight outward curve near the bottom of the pedestal, the pointed finial, and the number and size of the crenelations and vent holes. All these together certainly confirm the Minton attribution. (A gilded teapot, without pedestal, like the one at the Vic-

Fig. 21. Minton, c. 1817. Victoria and Albert Museum, London.

toria and Albert Museum, is in the Godden Collection.)

Rockingham also may have made porcelain tea warmers, c. 1820-42. The pedestal of one piece so attributed, seen some years ago in London, is oval shaped, with decoration of painted polychrome birds and gilt.

Miniature tea warmers of Derby porcelain, 1810-48, about 3 inches high, with a painted circular mark "Bloor Derby" in vermillion, have pedestals in the form of the conventional tower veilleuses with beaded upper rim and standing on a separate base that contains a small circular *godet*. The pedestals, teapots, *godets*, and bases are of various solid ground colors, undecorated except for gilt trim. Two such Derby miniatures are in the Jarvis Collection, New York City, one light blue and the other apple-green. There are two in the Newman Collection, one (complete) dark green and the other (lacking the teapot) apple-green.

# 4. France

Of all the known veilleuses, the majority by far are tea warmers made in France during the nineteenth century. Although tea was certainly not then an especially popular beverage in France, the explanation for the great quantity of veilleuse-théières was the French addiction to infusions (tisanes de camomille, de menthe, de tilleul) as nighttime or sickroom drinks. However, during the second half of the preceding century, before the introduction of the tea warmer, many potteries throughout France made food warmers (chauffe-nourriture) of faïence and of porcelain. But curiously the earliest known French veilleuses are for neither prepared food nor a beverage, but are unique in that, although they are basically in the form of the later tea warmers, the pot has no spout or handle; in fact, they are coquetières or egg boilers.

These pieces, the finest as well as the oldest known French veilleuses, are of Sèvres pâte tendre, 1758-59. The three known examples are all now located in England. One, with the date letter "F" for 1758, in the Wallace Collection, London, and often pictured, has a square pedestal (with no handles, masks, or even air vents), an octagonal pot (with slits on the shoulders for escaping steam), a circular godet, and a cover surmounted by a brown nesting hen with three white chicks; the whole piece has an apple-green ground with gilt trim and reserves of polychrome cartels of an amorino and trophies.[81] Another such Sèvres coquetière, in the Rothschild Collection, Waddesdon Manor, Aylesbury, Eng-

land, has a similarly modeled square pedestal (dated "G" for 1759), octagonal pot, and circular godet, all decorated on a bleu-de-roi ground with cartels of polychrome landscapes; the finial on the domed cover is a flower. (Plate I.) A third similar complete Sèvres coquetière, in the private collection of the Countess of Rosebery, Mentmore, Leighton Buzzard, England, has an apple-green ground with reserves of polychrome landscapes and figures, and a landscaped cover with no finial; it is dated "G" for 1759 and has an unidentified painter's mark "K."

There is no Sèvres veilleuse in the Musée Céramique de Sèvres nor any known in any other museum. Several Sèvres veilleuses are in private collections, and others certainly existed (including one sold in 1762 to Mme. de Pompadour).[82] Numerous veilleuses with various adaptations of Sèvres marks are known, but certainly they are not authentic and most probably they were made in Paris or Limoges, relatively recently.

The pedestal and cover (lacking the bowl) of a Sèvres pâte tendre food warmer, c. 1770-71, is in the Newman Collection. (Plate III.) The large cylindrical pedestal (diameter, 6¾ inches) has a wide aperture, and the modeling, showing the transition from rococo to neo-classical, includes two uplifted angular loop handles and two angular ribbed hooded vents. The decoration, floral sprays in cobalt blue with gilt bands bordered by blue feathering, is by the same hand as a plate and a bowl ("jatte en forme de cul de poule") in the Sèvres

56

Museum. The mark is interlaced LL's (without a date letter) surmounted by a simple line crown (not the royal crown used on Sèvres hard-paste porcelain); it is perhaps the mark of Sioux *aîné*, a Sèvres painter of flowers and borders from 1752 to 1792.

A hard-paste porcelain tea warmer in the Broulard collection was made at Sèvres, having workman's initials and factory mark on three parts showing that it was modeled there in "*1832 du 9ᵉ mois.*" (Fig. 22.) It is in the form of a design (reproduced on page 58) shown in a *livre tarif avec formes* made at the Sèvres factory during the First Empire (1800-15) for use by Director Alexandre Brongniart and other *Chefs de Service*, the book being now in the Sèvres Library. The pedestal is cylindrical and near its upper rim are air vents in the form of encircling pierced six-pointed stars (the stars in the design are five-pointed); it is decorated with a formal design, the ogives being painted (at a later date, and not at Sèvres) in *bleu-de-roi* on a white ground. The teapot and *bain-marie* are recessed entirely within the pedestal so that only the flame-like finial on the cover shows. The pedestal, teapot, *bain-marie*, and cover are identical to the design mentioned, except for a slight difference in the shape of the aperture and the number of points on the stars. These two differences are explained by another sketch in the Sèvres Library, dated June 1, 1832, and signed by Director A. Brongniart, which refers to corrections made as to the April 6, 1810, design of the "*Lampe veilleuse autel*" and shows the stars with six points and the changed aperture.

The sheet from the above-mentioned *livre tarif* shows designs for three veilleuses, with details of the separate parts of each. The first is the one above-described, with the complete piece shown, then the *bain-marie*, the teapot, and the *godet*. Next there is a veilleuse where the pitcher-shaped pot seems to be inserted to fit inside the large bowl; the *godet* seems to fit as a drawer with a front shield and a pull handle. The third is the most elaborate, an ovoid piece with a pitcher-shaped pot and the *godet* both presumably intended to fit inside the main

Fig. 22. Sèvres, 1832. Broulard Collection.

57

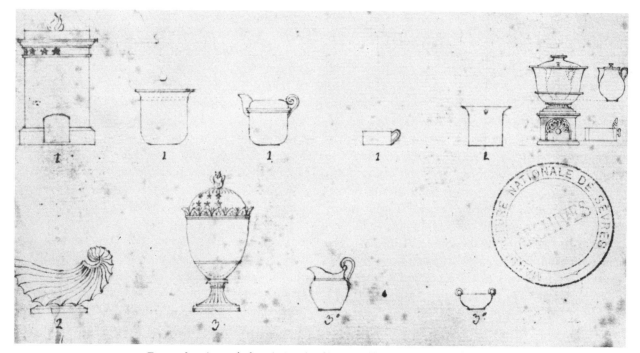

Reproduction of sketch in the *livre-tarif avec formes* of the Sèvres factory, now at the Sèvres Library. Photograph by Manufacture Nationale de Sèvres.

part; a separate water-color drawing of this third piece, also in the Sèvres Library and made by a porcelain designer named Bodson who worked at the Sèvres factory from 1813 to 1818, shows the intended decoration, with veiled nudes dancing around an encircling frieze and an owl as a finial above a field of stars on the domed cover. No example of the second or third models is known, although the records at Sèvres indicate that three examples of the third model were decorated by a porcelain painter named Jean-Charles Develly who painted at Sèvres 1813-1848.

Another hard-paste tea warmer made at Sèvres, identical in form with the Broulard piece (Fig. 22), is in the Newman Collection, with the standard factory date mark 1856 in chrome green and decoration mark *"Doré à Sèvres 1856"* in red; the piece lacks the pot within the *bain-marie*. The decoration, perhaps not done at Sèvres, is a yellow ground and an encircling reserved center white band with polychrome flowers. A hard-paste Sèvres food warmer, of the Louis Philippe period, in the Berthelot Collection, is different from the two described in that a

tall cylindrical bowl rests on the top of the cylindrical pedestal, both parts being white with gilt bands and edging; the pedestal has two angular loop handles and the bowl has two grooved knob handles. (Fig. 23.) The pedestal bears two standard Sèvres marks with the date 1847, the modeler's mark in underglaze chrome green and the decorator's mark in gilt.

Several early food warmers of faïence are from Niderviller, in Lorraine. A conically-shaped pedestal, c. 1760, in the Musée de Strasbourg (Château des Rohan), is larger than the pedestal of the average veilleuse (about 10 inches high); it has four hooded vents (instead of the usual two vents and two handles) and is decorated with polychrome flowers on a white ground. A very similar Niderviller food warmer, with the bowl having two flat handles but lacking the cover, is in the Museum für angewandte Kunst, Vienna. A complete Niderviller food warmer by Joseph Hannong, c. 1770, in the Strasbourg Museum, has polychrome flowers on a white ground, two hooded vents, and two yellow lion's-head mask handles; its unique feature is a 12-inch conforming plate *en suite*

Fig. 23. Sèvres, 1847. René Berthelot Collection, Paris.

Fig. 24. Niderviller, c. 1770. Joseph Hannong, Château des Rohan (Musée de Strasbourg), Strasbourg.

on which it rests.[83] (Fig. 24.) The pedestal of a Niderviller food warmer, 1760-70, in the Musée de Sèvres, has two yellow lion's-head mask handles and is decorated with flowers *en camaïeu* (dark red) on a white ground. Another Niderviller pedestal, marked "H" for Joseph Hannong, is in the Broulard Collection; it has like form and floral decoration. In the Victoria and Albert Museum (Stuart Davis Collection) there is a Niderviller food warmer of tin-glazed earthenware of the Custine period, 1770-84, decorated in enamel colors with a landscape *en camaïeu* (iron red) on an ivory ground and with two handles of lion's-head masks in yellow; the pedestal, unlike the usual cylindrical or slightly conical ones, is pyriform.[84] (Fig. 25.)

Very similar to the Niderviller models is a complete Strasbourg eighteenth-century food warmer in the Musée de Cluny, Paris; it is slightly conically shaped, with two handles in the form of sheep's-head masks, two hooded vents, and decoration of bouquets in characteristic purple of Cassius.[85]

Faïence food warmers of conventional shape, with slightly conical pedestals, were made in other regions of France. One from Sceaux, late eighteenth century, has animal-head masks in violet, polychrome floral decoration, a cherry finial, and a conforming *godet*.[86] One from Nevers (marked "Nevers 4 Avril 1797"), with handles of fruit in relief and decorated with medieval landscapes *en camaïeu* (brown-orange), is curious in that the aperture for the *godet* has a small door on metal hinges and a latch.[87] A piece from Lyons, marked 1765, with two covered warming bowls and a polychrome floral decoration, is in the Musée Historique de Lyon.[88] A faïence food warmer from the pottery of Veuve Perrin, Marseilles, c. 1770, in the Gandur Collection, has chinoiserie decoration, from a design by the engraver Jean Pillement, in polychrome on a white ground; its pedestal has four hooded vents and the bowl, tapering upward and outward from the pedestal, has two handles.[89] (Fig. 26.) An eighteenth-century faïence food warmer from Meillonas is in a French private collection.

Also probably from the eighteenth century is a faïence food warmer from Moustiers, in the Broulard Collection. (Fig. 27.) It is of conventional shape, but smaller than the usual food warmers. It has an exceptionally large aperture, two cat's-mask handles, two hooded vents, and a conforming *godet*. The bowl has two lateral handles (broken). Its decoration, blue on a bluish ground, consists of a lattice and floral pattern, with several painted mosquitoes. The interior of the pedestal has wreathing similar to the English delft food warmers.

Most unusual in form are several identically modeled glazed earthenware food warmers from Sarreguemines (Moselle), made by Utzschneider et Cie., 1810-20. They are shaped like circular Grecian urns set on a square plinth which contains the *godet*. The domed cover of the urn has a finial in the form of an owl. They have no decoration except the modeling, which features a pierced scroll design around the urn for ventilation. Three such pieces are colored rare *carmélite*; they are, respectively, in the Château des Rohan, Strasbourg[90] (Fig 28), the Musée Historique Lorrain, Nancy, and the Saarlandmuseum, Saarbrücken. Another piece in this form (lacking the bowl), but of a later date, c. 1830-40, is cream-colored; it is in the Broulard Collection.

Quite in contrast is an Alsatian food-warmer pedestal in the Musée d'Unterlinden, Colmar, France. Of *terre vernissée,* c. 1820, and crudely decorated with black and brown dots on a beige ground, it is pyriform, with two small loop handles and a hooded vent.

A food warmer whose pedestal has sloping sides, two ear-shaped loop handles and two hooded vents and whose decoration is an overall marbled blue and white pattern, is in the Brosio Collection; it is attributed to Vienne, France, c. 1780. (Fig. 29.) Very similar in form are three undecorated milky-white faïence food warmers in the Broulard Collection from potteries in Burgundy: two of them (Fig. 30) have similar hooded vents and thick ear-shaped loop handles on the pedestal, and the covered bowls have uplifted protruding flat handles (a similar piece is in the Musée des Hospices, Lyons, France, and another is in the Newman Collection); the other, with tassel-shaped hoods over the vents, has one pedestal but both an *écuelle* and a *théière* (comparable to the interchangeable model shown in the 1817 *Wedgwood Queen's Ware Catalogue*).

Other undecorated glazed faïence food warmers were made in many places in France in the late eighteenth century. One of cream color in conventional form, but unidentified, is in the Musée des Arts Décoratifs, Paris. Two in the Broulard Collection (Fig. 31) and one in the

Fig. 25. Niderviller, 1770-84. Victoria and Albert Museum, London.

Fig. 26. Marseilles, Veuve Perrin, c. 1770. Gandur Collection.

Fig. 27. Moustiers, late eighteenth century. Broulard Collection.

Fig. 28. Sarreguemines (Moselle). Utzschneider et Cie., c. 1810-20. Château des Rohan (Musée de Strasbourg), Strasbourg.

Fig. 29. Vienne, France, c. 1780. Brosio Collection, Museo Civico, Turin.

66

Fig. 30. Burgundy, c. 1780-90. "Animated Conversation."
Broulard Collection.

67

68

Fig. 31. Creil, creamware, 1770-90. Broulard Collection.

Newman Collection, all cream-colored and very similar and all bearing the impressed mark "Creil" (which pottery imitated English Queen's Ware), have two bell-shaped hooded vents and two handles of open-mouth animal masks; a like piece is in the Museo Civico, Turin, Italy. Also in the Broulard Collection are two undecorated food warmers with bell-shaped hooded vents and with large jug-shaped pots, one being white-cream colored from Moustiers and one yellow from Beauvais. This collection also has one severe, slightly conical food warmer of faïence from Lyons whose bowl has two flat lateral handles; its interesting feature is a pair of knob-like side handles which have center holes as air vents and which are grooved so that, presumably, a wire overhead carrying handle may be attached.

Food warmers of undecorated glazed faïence were also made at Apt, in the Vaucluse near Aix-en-Provence. The body was buff color, with a yellow lead glaze that was prone to crazing. Characteristic Apt features of modeling are rectangular apertures for the *godet*, small beading around the pedestal, and tassel-shaped hoods over the air vents (although sometimes there are masks over the vents). An Apt food warmer (impressed "Apt" and "Lamy") in the Broulard Collection is of conventional Apt form, the pedestal having two tassel-shaped hooded vents and a rectangular aperture, and the bowl having two flat lateral handles. A comparable piece (similarly impressed) in the Newman Collection has a jug-shaped pot in addition to the bowl. Such jug-shaped pots made at Apt are similar to the Beauvais and Moustiers pieces already described; characteristic of these pieces are pouring lips instead of spouts and a cover with two small holes so that it can be tied to the pot handle by a bit of string. Five such pieces in somewhat varying form are in the Berthelot Collection, and two are in the Newman Collection.

A brown-glazed faïence food warmer of uncertain provenance and date, but probably late eighteenth century, in the Berthelot Collection, has two grooved knob handles on its pedestal, and above the aperture and on the reverse are male masks which, with their prominent chins and sharply molded features, resemble the English delft masks. (Fig. 32.) The interior of the pedestal has wreathing also similar to the delftware pieces. The jug-shaped pot resembles those described above.

An interesting unmarked food warmer of tawny creamware, crazed from heat (especially the *godet* which has become brownish in color), is in the collection of Old Sturbridge Village, Sturbridge, Massachusetts.[91] (Fig. 33.) The pedestal is cylindrical, but one-third of the way up it reduces about ½ inch in radius. At its sides are relief female-head masks with ornate headdresses, and just below the masks are channeled air vents. The bowl has two flat lateral handles and a cover with a knob finial. All parts have encircling bands of small beaded decoration. Identical pieces are in the Berthelot and Newman Collections. The piece at Sturbridge has been attributed there to Wedgwood, but the body, form, and decoration certainly negate its being Wedgwood or even English. The more likely provenance is indicated by comparison with a piece in the Broulard Collection which is of reddish *terre cuite* glazed dark brown. (Fig. 34.) This piece has a cylindrical pedestal which, although smaller, is of identical shape to that of the Sturbridge piece, with identical three-point scalloped aperture and encircling beaded bands and vent holes. Instead of a bowl, it has a jug-shaped pot (like the food warmers from Moustiers, Beauvais, and Apt described above) with curved handle and pouring lip. Despite the differences in form and body, this piece indicates that the Sturbridge food warmer (and the other two like it) also probably came from Apt or nearby in Provence.

A few food warmers of porcelain were made in France during the same period of the late eighteenth century. In the Bowes Museum, at Barnard Castle in northern England, there is one of *porcelaine de la Reine*, Rue Thiroux, Paris, 1778-90, of usual cylindrical shape, with *décor à barbeaux* (blue cornflowers), characteristic of this factory, on a white ground and with two lion's-head mask handles. (Fig. 35.) A similar piece (cover missing) from the same factory, with the mark of a large "A" (for Marie Antoinette, patron of the factory) in red below a royal crown, is in the Newman Collection; it has similar mask handles and hooded vents, and is decorated with an overall pattern of small purple and red-and-yellow flowers.

A porcelain food warmer from Lorraine, 1780-90, of conventional cylindrical form but decorated in *trompe l'oeil sur fond bois* in the style commonly associated with Niderviller, is in the Château des Rohan,

Fig. 32. France. Brown-glazed earthenware, c. 1800.
Georges Berthelot Collection, Paris.

Fig. 33. France (?). Creamware. Collection of Old Sturbridge Village, Sturbridge, Massachusetts.

Fig. 34. France (?). Broulard Collection.

Fig. 35. Porcelaine de la Reine, Rue Thiroux, Paris, 1780-
90. Bowes Museum, Barnard Castle, Durham, England.

Strasbourg. It has "framed" pastoral scenes on the pedestal and the cover *en camaïeu* (black) on a burgundy ground, and has shell-shaped handles.

Some early French tea warmers were made of faïence. The earliest known example, c. 1760, and one of the few tea warmers antedating 1800, is of faïence of Marseilles, from the establishment of Veuve Perrin, which flourished in the latter part of the eighteenth century.[92] The pedestal is very similar in form to the conventional food warmers of Sceaux, Nevers, and Lyons already discussed; it is wide and slightly conical, has a hooded vent over the aperture and on the reverse, but has no handles. The upper part is a teapot whose sides carry upward the lines of the pedestal, very similar to the Wedgwood tea warmers. The decoration features polychrome Chinese figures. This piece shows the transition from the eighteenth-century food warmers to the nineteenth-century tea warmers. It has been called a "unique object of its kind."[93]

Another eighteenth-century tea warmer of faïence of

73

**Fig. 36. Marseilles, 1754-93. Joseph-Gaspard Robert. Collection of Mme. Raoul Kraft, Geneva.**

Marseilles is from the factory of Joseph-Gaspard Robert, 1754-93. It is of rather similar shape, with a wide cylindrical pedestal having two hooded vents and a conforming teapot extending conically upward the lines of the pedestal. It is decorated with cartouches of trophies *en* *camaïeu* (dark green) and with black borders on a white ground. (Fig. 36.) This rare veilleuse is in the Kraft Collection, Geneva.[94]

No other eighteenth-century French tea warmer is known, but a reproduction of a catalogue of a shop in

74

Fig. 37. Apt, c. 1780-90. Broulard Collection.

La Rochelle, France, 1779, lists "3 veilleuses,"[95] which term might have referred to tea warmers rather than to food warmers.

Faïence tea warmers in yellow-colored glazed earthenware were made at Apt in the early nineteenth century. They are similar in form to the Apt food warmers, but two in the Broulard Collection are significantly different. One, with a wide cylindrical pedestal and characteristic-ally having a rectangular aperture and two tassel-shaped handles, has a teapot shaped like the Perrin model from Marseilles. The other, whose similarly modeled pedestal has encircling beading, has a high pot with an animalistic spout. (Fig. 37.)

A tea warmer of cream-colored glazed earthenware, in the form of the conventional Wedgwood tea warmers, with two large loop handles and the same pierced leafage

Fig. 38. Paris (?). Broulard Collection.

decoration, and bearing the impressed mark "Chamot Fr. & Cie." on the pedestal, is in the Broulard Collection.

From Creil after 1800 came faïence tea warmers as well as the cream-colored glazed earthenware food warmers described above. A popular model marked "Creil et Montereau" (which pottery operated from 1819 to 1895) has a low bulbous pedestal and teapot with vertical fluting. One such piece, in the Broulard Collection, is decorated with polychrome cherry-blossom sprays, and another with alternate fluting of silver luster. A veilleuse similarly modeled in the Freed Collection has polychrome floral decoration.

Three faïence tea warmers in the Berthelot Collection, all similarly modeled, are marked *"Terre d'Acier. Saint Uze."* They are glazed gray-white, with decoration of floral sprays outlined in blue. One such piece has a *bain-marie.*

Porcelain tea warmers were made in France during the nineteenth century in great quantity and innumerable forms. Examples too numerous for description are in the Berthelot, Broulard, Chiavassa, Freed, Gandur, and Kraft Collections. The most frequently seen French model has a teapot resting on a pedestal in the shape of a circular tower which stands on a separate base; these were made with the upper rim of the tower either crenelated or beaded. The crenelated tower, usually of finer and more translucent porcelain, was also made in other countries. An interesting beaded tower, in the Broulard Collection, has a teapot of unusual shape and has the air vents of the pedestal in the gallery at the top rather than at the customary place on the outside; the decoration of this piece is a Scottish landscape with kilted figures. (Fig. 38.)

A porcelain tea warmer made by Jacques-Louis Chalot, at Chantilly, c. 1833, is interesting, not only for its unusual form but due to the fact that it won for the modeler a silver medal at the Paris Exposition of Industrial Products, 1834, in recognition of its being the first piece of porcelain that used a new mechanical process, in lieu of hand modeling or molding, to make the gadroon bands and the palm-leaf finial.[96] The pedestal, on a separate base, has a dodecagonal form, with 12 narrow vertical panels, and the teapot conforms. The entire piece is white. It is in the Sèvres Museum.

Before further discussion of French tea warmers made of porcelain, mention must be made of Jacob Petit (b. 1796), the French ceramist whose name is most frequently connected with veilleuses. In 1815 Jacob Petit became associated with a pottery in Rue Ferrare, at Fontainebleau, owned by Benjamin Jacob and Aaron Smoll, which had started hard-paste manufacture about 1795. In 1830 the business was bought by Jacob Petit and his brother Mardochée, and in 1834 it was moved to another factory that he had acquired in 1820 in Rue Basse-Saint-Denis, at Belleville, in Paris. His pieces bore the mark "J.P." (variously written) in underglaze blue or occasionally incised. Having moved his factory again in 1851 to nearby Avon, he sold it in 1862 to an employee named Jacquemin, and in 1863 he opened a new factory in Rue Paradis-Poissonière, Paris. Jacquemin and his successors (Raingo, Violatte, and Charon) continued to operate the Avon factory with great success, and they continued to use the purchased Jacob Petit models, molds, and marks until after 1886.[97] It has been suggested that some of the pieces were made in white glaze at Limoges and there marked in underglaze, and then later were decorated at the factories of Jacob Petit and his successors.[98] This recital clearly suggests uncertainty as to the origin and date of some pieces attributed to Jacob Petit, even some bearing his mark.

It is recognized that Jacob Petit was the leader of the Romantic School of French porcelain which commenced about 1830. Reacting vigorously against the severity of the Empire Period, it deliberately broke all restraints, creating capricious lines and rococo decoration, as well as using vivid colors and much gilt. The influence of Jacob Petit was very great and many factories, not only in France, followed his example, although often without his flair, spontaneity, or skill, thus committing many excesses.[99]

Some of the treatises on ceramics, especially those by English writers, give Jacob Petit scant notice. It has been said of the Jacob Petit factory that after 1830 it "became very prosperous, making crude and showy wares"[100] which were "of little artistic merit,"[101] and that "only wares of commercial standing were produced, many being in the 19th-century revived rococo style,"[102] and "the production is not bad as to execution, but unhappily it is the models which are of a deplorable taste, the responsibility for which rests less on the maker than the epoch in which he lived."[103] More caustically, "Dresden models and style of decoration were copied. The production of this manufactory are not much sought after save by dealers, who buy them mainly for the American decorators' market."[104] But recently the high quality of his porcelain, his modeling, and his coloring, especially in the case of his figures, has been recognized by French writers.[105]

Notwithstanding the derogatory remarks, most French antique dealers proudly (and at expensive prices) display pieces bearing his mark, or even attributed, on the basis of form, decoration, and coloring, to his factory. And in any event the veilleuses of Jacob Petit (and particularly those bearing his underglaze blue initials) are the French tea warmers most sought and prized by the vast majority of private collectors today.

Among the porcelain tea warmers of basic circular shape modeled and decorated by Jacob Petit, one model is particularly characteristic of his lavish style. The pedestal has an elaborate encircling crown and overhanging valance, and the teapot has a conforming upper rim. Several known examples have different ground colors and decoration, but all are richly painted and have much gold encrustation. One such signed piece, in the Newman Collection, is of *bleu céleste* ground with encircling reserves decorated with polychrome garlands, and its base, crown, and valance are pale peach. (Plate IV.) Another, in the same collection, has black ground and polychrome jewel decoration. One in the Freed Collection has a black ground with encrusted floral decoration, and the base, crown, and valance are green and gold. There are four such pieces in the Chiavassa Collection, all of different color and decoration, but equally ornate. Very closely related to this Jacob Petit model is another by him that has an identical teapot but the pedestal is pyriform with a spreading crown; one signed piece is in the Brosio Collection, Museo Civico, Turin (Fig. 39) and there are several signed specimens in the Chiavassa Collection. An unsigned veilleuse with an identically modeled teapot but whose pedestal is mounted in ormulu is in the Freed Collection; as it has no separate porcelain base with air holes, there are three small holes in the bottom of the pedestal, whose lack of any aperture would make the insertion of the *godet* from the top most impracticable.

Most of the *personnages* are attributed to the workmanship or design of Jacob Petit. An outstanding signed example, said to be typical of the *"curieuse inspiration propre"* of Jacob Petit, is in the Musée Céramique de Rouen. The figure is a lady of the court of Louis XVI in a very elegant and colorful dress and with a plumed headdress, seated atop a gilded round pedestal and holding in her hands a small teapot (which is the spout of the veilleuse).[106] A similar signed piece is in the Brosio Collection,[107] one is in the Berthelot Collection, two are in the Chiavassa Collection, and another is in the Freed Collection; and in the Newman Collection there is also a similar signed piece except that the small teapot is round instead of rectangular as in the other six examples.[108] (Fig. P–1.) This model is in the only known *personnage* whose figure rests on such a separate high and imposing pedestal (making it doubly impracticable by placing the bottom of the teapot so far above the flame of the *godet* within the pedestal).

The fact that the above-described veilleuse is the only *personnage* known to be in any museum (other than those in the Brosio Collection recently acquired by the Museo Civico, Turin) may attest to the scarcity of such pieces now outside private collections rather than support the above-quoted belittling comments regarding the work of Jacob Petit, especially as the Musée des Arts Décoratifs, Paris, and other museums in France and elsewhere do display vases, clocks, and other porcelain objects made by him.

Usually the *personnage* veilleuses* are in the form of figures, male and female, standing or seated, wearing a variety of regional attire. (Fig. 40.) Among them are so-called "marquises" of the French court, Madame Du Barry (Plate V), nuns and monks, Oriental sultans and sultanas, Chinese mandarins and mandarinesses (Plate VI), Zouaves and gladiators, hunters and musketeers (Plate VII), Spanish dancers and Breton peasants, girls with a mandolin, lyre, bagpipe, fan, watering pail, or letter, St. Vincent de Paul and St. Cecilia.[109] (Figs. P-1 to P-91.)

---

*Note: Most of the *personnages* and architectural veilleuses discussed in this chapter are of uncertain provenance; but as the great majority of them certainly were made in France (a few have been attributed to Italy but none has been positively so identified), the entire discussion is included in this chapter.

Fig. 39. France. Jacob Petit. Brosio Collection, Museo Civico, Turin.

Fig. 40. *Personnage.* Girl carrying basket and jar. (Two models.) Newman Collection. (See Fig. P-23.)

Many *personnages* recur in the identical costume and colors, but some figures similarly modeled are variously colored, such as the two marquises (Figs. P–2 and P–3) and the peasant girl carrying a basket (Fig. 40 and Fig. P–23). In some such cases the same factory may have indulged in the variation of decoration, and in fact the Jacob Petit mark does sometimes appear on several versions of the same *personnage* (such as Fig. P–1). But Jacob Petit is said to have decorated only a few of his productions[110] and, if his figures were sold in white to outside decorators, that may explain some unsigned examples of the identical figure with varied colors and even style of costume. In other cases, the same figure varies in modeling details, such as the girl holding aloft the bunch of grapes (Fig. P–24 and Fig. P–25), and these may have been products of the same factory but a different repairer, or of an itinerant modeler working at different potteries; another possibility is that the original figure may have been used as a model elsewhere, just as many porcelain figures not veilleuses were often copied or adapted far from the original factory. The consequent difficulty in making attributions of the *personnages* becomes apparent.

A few *personnages* bear the underglaze blue mark of Jacob Petit (some in rather dubious form). Probably most of these are the work, as to both modeling and decoration, of this innovator who revived the Romantic style in French ceramics, although some may be the products of the successors at his factory who took over his models and molds. But it may also be that some such pieces were modeled or decorated by later imitators or copyists.

Several types of *personnages* have been recorded but their whereabouts now is not known, nor any like models. They were sold on July 6, 1931 at auction at the Hôtel Drouot, Paris, among 127 veilleuses (including 49 different *personnages*) belonging to that famed Parisian courtesan, Mme. Emilienne d'Alençon.[111] These included a Madonna holding the Child in her left arm and a palm in her right hand; a kneeling woman supporting a star-covered globe encircled by signs of the zodiac; an apothecary holding a syringe; a girl eating cakes from a drum-shaped canister; an Oriental girl with a dagger; a Norman woman taking snuff; a Spanish girl carrying an urn on her right shoulder; and a matched pair representing a hunter extending a cup to his companion as she pours from a pitcher.[111-A] Another recorded model of which no example is now known is the dolphin ridden by Neptune, later mentioned.

Religious motifs occasionally were a part of the decoration of tea warmer veilleuses. In addition, a few *personnages* depicted religious characters, such as the two versions of the Madonna and Child (one is shown in Fig. P–45). The pedestal of an unusual tea warmer has in front a grotto in which stands the figure of the Virgin and Child, and at her feet is a small font for Holy Water. (Fig. 41.) The Brosio Collection has a simple veilleuse with an hexagonal pedestal, white with gilt bands, that also has a small projecting font.

A type of veilleuse related to the *personnages* is in the form of an animal, real or grotesque, the upper half of which is a teapot. A rare and fantastic specimen is an elephant squatting on its haunches. (Fig. P–63.) Another elephant *personnage* has the elephant standing erect and wearing a man's suit of many colors. (Fig. P–64.) In this group is a fox dressed as a *Garde du Village* and stealing a goose. (Fig. P–65.)

Related to these animal *personnages* are hybrid *personnages* which have an undivided animal supporting a conventional teapot. Such a piece is a standing elephant surmounted by a howdah (the teapot); stated to be in the Emilio Terry Collection, it has been described as of hard paste of Paris, c. 1840, with the elephant and the black mahout (with turban and loin cloth) astride his neck, both in natural colors, the elephant being covered with a tasseled carpet of dark rose and gold.[112] It is in the style of Jacob Petit and, although unsigned, was perhaps from his factory. A similarly modeled elephant veilleuse, with slight variations in the decoration (Fig. P–66), and another elephant veilleuse, but without the mahout (Fig. P–67), are in the Brosio Collection at Turin. An elephant veilleuse somewhat similar to those described but with the mahout as the lid of the teapot is in the Chiavassa Collection. A comparable veilleuse is in the form of a sitting camel whose howdah is the teapot. (Fig. P–68.)

Sometimes the teapot rather than the pedestal is in the form of an animal. One such piece has a pot in the shape of a duck. (Fig. P–69.) Occasionally a conventionally modeled teapot veilleuse is decorated with animals in

Fig. 41. France. Tea warmer with holy water font. Broulard Collection.

relief, such as one with three drinking monkeys[113] (Fig. P–70), or with a human figure in relief. (Plate VIII.)

There are numerous examples of *personnage* veilleuses in the form of a grotesque beast with fangs and a very long snout, squatting on its hind legs on a rococo base and holding in front a shield depicting a variety of scenes, several showing figures in Hades. (Fig. P–71.) A somewhat different form of grotesque *personnage* (Plate IX) is a very colorful squatting figure, part human and part animal, holding two large fish; the teapot is the head, with side whiskers and uplifted nose (the spout), and the cover is modeled with a conforming grotesque long-nosed face.[114]

A particularly ornate and prized type of *personnage* depicts a dolphin, very richly colored, on which rides Amphitrite holding a ewer (Plate X and Fig. P–73) or Neptune with a horn of plenty[115] (no existing example is now known), the teapot being the upper half of the figure. A comparable *personnage* very often seen is a young Bacchus riding a goat, with many vari-colored fruits and vegetables on the base.[116] (Fig. P–74.) Related to this group are dolphins ridden by Triton holding a trident[117] (Fig. P–75) or blowing a conch horn (Fig. P–76) or by a winged Cupid[118] (Fig. P–77). Other such pieces are a swan ridden by Cupid (Fig. P–78) and a rather voluptuous mermaid with upraised arms supporting a shell-shaped teapot on her head (Fig. P–79). All these last five models are hybrid *personnages* in that the teapot is not a part of the figure but a conventional teapot integrated into the veilleuse.

Another hybrid type of *personnage* combines the conventional tea warmer with a figure, placing the teapot on a small pedestal with the figure or figures standing in front, behind, or alongside. (Figs. P–80, P–81, and P–82). One such model, with a man standing behind a peepshow upon which rests a teapot, has been made with variations in the number of children clustered around the peepshow; they range from two to four. (Fig. P-83). Another such veilleuse depicts a Roman gladiator with a sword standing in front of a pedestal supporting the teapot (Fig. P-84), and a companion piece is a Roman matron (Fig. P-85). A very rare veilleuse of this type has, standing beside a pedestal supporting a teapot, a colorful figure of Nostradamus wearing a high conical hat and reading from a cabalistic book.[119] (Fig. P-86.)

Occasionally *personnages* are found in white glaze. (Fig. P–89.) This is usually because the piece has a fire crack and was rejected by the decorator or was made at one factory to be decorated elsewhere. But it may have been because the modeler dared, as did Jacob Petit at times, to leave the piece undecorated so that he could better display the perfection of his modeling skill.[120] Two known white-glazed models are made of very hard porcelain with a thick glaze that veils the features of the figures. (Figs. P–90 and P–91.)

A wholly different type of teapot veilleuse is classified as architectural. An ornately modeled and frequently seen example is the cathedral of porcelain from Limoges, 1830-43, a specimen of which is in the Musée Adrien Dubouché, Limoges. (Fig. 42.) The pedestal is in the form of a rectangular Gothic cathedral, with small spires at the four corners and a rose window on each side. The whole piece is usually white with gilt decoration, but one with peach ground is in the Kraft Collection, one with pale green ground is in the Freed Collection, and a handsome polychrome example is in the Berthelot Collection.

Another Romantic type of architectural veilleuse is related to the cathedral but omits the spires and other modeling details. These (sometimes called "*style cathédrale*") generally have hexagonal pedestals with two large opposite panels and four narrow end panels. The panels are of *vitrail* design, the upper part having relief Gothic arches and rose windows. The teapot, not a part of the cathedral design, is usually of conforming shape and decoration. An example, c. 1830, in the Le Tallec Collection, has the characteristic arcading and rose tracery, with grilles painted and in relief around the upper rim of the pedestal; it is decorated with formal polychrome birds and flowers in the style of the pre-Romantic period.[121] Another such piece, with colorful paintings on the two large panels, is in the Broulard Collection (Fig. 43), three are in the Freed Collection, one is in the Berthelot Collection, and several are in the Chiavassa Collection. One in the Brosio Collection, much larger than usual but whose pedestal and teapot are almost identically modeled, has been attributed to Ginori, c. 1835-40[122]; a similar veilleuse is in the Freed Collection.

A veilleuse of similar type, but with the pedestal having six equal sides, is the only tea warmer in the Musée

Fig. 42. Cathedral. Limoges, 1830-40. Musée Adrien Dubouché, Limoges, France.

Fig. 43. France. Hexagonal with two large panels. Freed
Collection.

des Arts Décoratifs, Paris. (Fig. 44.) It was formerly attributed by the museum to Jacob Petit, but it is now considered as having been made by the pottery of Bastien et Bugeard, 95 Faubourg St.-Martin, Paris, 1830-50 (many pieces from that factory having been donated to the museum in 1922 by M. Charles Bastien). Its hexagonal pedestal has alternating panels of polychrome scenic cartels and *vitrail* design on a green ground, and its teapot has cartouches of cherubs.[123] Comparable *vitrail* veilleuses with equisided hexagonal pedestals are in the Berthelot, Broulard, Brosio, Chiavassa, Freed (Fig. 45), and Newman Collections. A regular hexagonal tea warmer of white-glazed *terre de pipe* from Gien, France (Geoffroy et Cie.), c. 1855, in the Newman Collection, has six Gothic arches in the usual cathedral style.

Especially ornamental is the type of veilleuse whose pedestal, while also hexagonal in shape, has three alternating sides wider than the intervening ones; the teapot, conforming in shape, is usually gilded. The three wide panels (sometimes slightly concave) have paintings of Biblical or operatic scenes or some romantic episodes; the narrow panels usually are of *vitrail* design. There are three such pieces in the Freed Collection, one in the Broulard Collection, and one in the Newman Collection. (Fig. 46.)

A related group of tea warmers has regular octagonal pedestals. The Freed Collection has one such piece ornately modeled and marked "Darte, Palais-Royale No. 21"; its pedestal has Gothic arches and scenic panels. (Fig. 47.) Three others so shaped, but in pagoda style with Chinese motifs, are also in the Freed Collection. An interesting variation in the Kraft Collection has one panel of its octagonal pedestal modeled as a projecting stairway. Another veilleuse with a regular octagonal pedestal, in the Essex Institute, Salem, Massachusetts, has an unusual salmon-colored ground with alternate salmon panels decorated with a shell and gilding and white panels decorated with polychrome flowers.

A rarer variation of this group has three large panels separated by very narrow gilded strips, so that the piece is really triangular with chamfered corners. An example, called a "*Lampe de Malade*," was decorated c. 1825 by Marc and Victor Schoelcher in Paris; the upper part of the pedestal (which rests on a conforming base, as this type of tea warmer always does, and so has no aperture) has Gothic arches in relief, and the three panels and the teapot are decorated with Oriental gilt floral motifs edged in black on a white ground.[124] There is one such piece in the Broulard Collection (Plate XI) and another in the Newman Collection.

Oval pedestals are also not often seen. These generally are decorated with encircling scenic paintings or with two large painted panels, and rest on a separate base (having no aperture to impinge upon the painting). Usually the porcelain is of fine translucent quality. A good example is in the Broulard Collection (Fig. 48), and there are others (some exceptionally large and richly decorated with gilt) in the Berthelot, Chiavassa, and Freed Collections.

Also infrequently found are veilleuses with sharply squared or rectangular pedestals. One with a square pedestal, ornately decorated, is in the Berthelot Collection (Fig. 49), and there are other square and rectangular pieces in the Berthelot, Broulard, Chiavassa, and Freed Collections.

A very elaborate tea warmer of the architectural type, in the Newman Collection, is unmarked but probably from Paris, c. 1814-30. (Plate XII.) It represents a Persian temple, with a rectangular pedestal having on one narrow end an arched aperture for a *godet,* a two-tiered roof with gilt chimneys, and at the corners lattice-work supports for the overhanging roof. The small conforming teapot is also rectangular, with two onion-topped corner spires on each side, and its roof-like cover has a crescent finial topped with a knob. The roofs and the teapot are *bleu céleste* with gold floral sprays, the valances are of gold filigree, and the walls and lattices have enameled pink roses and polychrome flowers on a white ground.

Another extravagant architectural tea warmer, in the Freed Collection, is in the form of a castle. (Fig. 50.) It bears the underglaze blue mark of Jacob Petit. At the four corners of the square pedestal are projecting round towers surmounted by crenelated turrets. The entire edifice, including the square crenelated teapot, is blue, with white windows framed in gilt. The base has a small stairway leading up to the portal on the pedestal. A similar piece in the Chiavassa Collection is white with polychrome floral sprays.

Also with the Jacob Petit mark is an architectural

Fig. 44. Hexagonal, *style cathédrale*. Bastien et Bugeard, Paris, 1830-50. Musée des Arts Décoratifs, Paris.

Fig. 45. France. Regular hexagonal and *vitrail*. Freed Collection.

Fig. 46. Hexagonal with concave panels. Newman Collection.

Fig. 47. Octagonal. Paris. Darte, Palais-Royale No. 21. Freed Collection.

Fig. 48. Oval. Broulard Collection.

Fig. 49. France. Square. Georges Berthelot Collection,
Paris.

Fig. 50. Castle. France, Jacob Petit. Freed Collection.

94    Fig. 51. Rustic chapel. France. Signed Jacob Petit. Broulard Collection.

veilleuse whose pedestal is in the form of a square rustic chapel with four relief trees at the corners as columns and all surmounted by a roof with dormer windows. The teapot, square and of conforming style, has windows like the pedestal and a pointed roof. Such a piece, with polychrome decoration, is in the Broulard Collection (Fig. 51) and another is in the Berthelot Collection. One in the Brosio Collection has its base, roof, and trees in brown, and the chapel in white with gilt and polychrome floral sprays.[125] A similar piece in the Freed Collection is white glazed with fire cracks; it has added encrusted flowers.

In this group of architectural tea warmers, but of inferior quality, is the veilleuse in the form of a Paris kiosk. (Fig. 52.) The hexagonal pedestal is variously decorated, and the dome-shaped teapot has a smokestack handle and a dormer-window spout. Three such pieces in the Freed Collection bear the same mark, "*Deposé*, H. J. & Cie., V." and presumably were made by Hache, Julien & Cie., Vierzon (Cher), France, 1885-93.

Comparable architectural veilleuses, probably late nineteenth century, are in the form of various rustic edifices, such as a windmill (Fig. 53), a thatched farmhouse, a stone mill (Fig. 54), a timbered cottage, a stone Alsatian mill (Fig. 55), a dovecote, a brick farmhouse, and a village hotel. An amusing model in the Broulard Collection depicts a lighthouse with a girl leaning out of the dormer window while her swain sings at the door below. (Fig. 56.)

A curious architectural veilleuse in the Newman Collection has its pedestal made of blackened bronze in the form of a square crenelated stone tower. It has gilded barred windows on three sides, and the fourth side is a drawbridge that descends on two chains and that carries outward on a swivel holder the glass *godet*. Above the windows and the drawbridge are gilded figures of knights in armor superimposed in grilled niches. The teapot is porcelain and entirely gilded. (Fig. 57.) A similar piece is in the Berthelot Collection.

Veilleuses of lusterware are not often seen. Two small teapot veilleuses in the Newman Collection are decorated with "silver" (platinum resist) luster, showing delicate floral designs in white outline; a similar veilleuse is in the Berthelot Collection. Another tea warmer in the Newman Collection is in the shape of an octagonal timbered

Fig. 52. Paris kiosk. Vierzon. Hache, Julien & Cie. Freed Collection.

Fig. 53. Windmill. "Moulin Joli." France. Newman Collection.

Fig. 54. Stone mill. Broulard Collection.

Fig. 55. France. Stone Alsatian mill. Newman Collection.

Fig. 56. Brick lighthouse. Broulard Collection.

Fig. 57. Bronze turret. Newman Collection.

cottage with figures at the doorway of a young girl supporting her inebriated companion; it is marked "G. B. & Cie., Paris" and was made by Gillet and Briançon, Rue Lafayette, Paris, c. 1855-60, of patented lusterware,[126] the entire piece being decorated in pastel colors. A similarly modeled piece is in the Freed Collection (Fig. 58) and there is also one in the Berthelot Collection, but they are of polychrome painted porcelain, not lusterware.

Lithophane, with its quality of showing its grisaille friezes to best advantage when illuminated from behind, would seem ideal for pedestals of veilleuses.[127] Surprisingly, such pieces are comparatively scarce. An exceptionally fine one, in the Broulard Collection, has a rectangular pedestal resting on a separate base; the teapot is unique in that it has two spouts. The pedestal has four gilded corner columns and a turreted upper rim; its four lithophane panels depict New Testament scenes. The glazed portion of the porcelain is *bleu céleste*. (Fig. 59.) An almost identical piece in the Freed Collection, but entirely white, with the "J.P." mark, has slight variations in the details of the modeling, and another, with gilt trim, is in the Blair Collection. Also in the Broulard Collection is another similar piece (the glazed columns differ), entirely white, but its teapot has only one spout and a comparably modeled handle opposite it.

Other lithophane veilleuses are of various shapes. One, circular and in the form of a chapel, has statues on the columns separating the four lithophane panels and has cherubs on the cornice and the base; such a piece is in the Blair Collection, at the Blair Museum of Lithophanes, Toledo, Ohio (Fig. 60), as well as the Broulard, Chiavassa, and Freed Collections. Another has a rectangular pedestal with gilt bands along the edges; an example, with the relief mark "A D T" (indicating that it was made by Baron A. de Tremblay, of Rubelles, France, whose factory made lithophanes from 1836 to 1858), is in the Newman Collection (Fig. 61) and another is in the Freed Collection. A third type, in the Brosio Collection, probably made in Italy by Ginori, c. 1870, has a bulbous round pedestal like other Ginori tea warmers[128]; similar pieces are in the Blair and Freed Collections.

The only known veilleuse model with a pentagonal pedestal has four of its sides made of large lithophane panels, the fifth side having the aperture for the *godet* below a small lithophane panel. One such piece, in the Blair Collection, is unmarked but the panels are similar to other lithophanes in that collection marked "A D T" for Baron A. de Tremblay. (Fig. 62.) The large panels not shown in the photograph depict a seated ballet dancer and a helmeted horseman. A similar lithophane veilleuse with different panels is in the Berthelot Collection.

Some lithophane veilleuses are modeled in the same form as certain porcelain tea warmers already described. One, with a triangular pedestal and chamfered corners, with three lithophane panels, is in the Freed Collection, and a similar piece, but with bands of blue and gilt, is in the Broulard Collection. Another is in the form of the hexagonal tea warmers with two large panels on opposite sides of the pedestal; such a piece, in the Blair Collection, has two large panels of lithophane and the other sides of porcelain with polychrome decoration.

Such transparencies, which date from 1827, are technically lithophanes only if the design is intaglio, i.e., recessed rather than raised (having been cast from molds made from wax models).[129] But some veilleuses are made of translucent white porcelain, glazed or biscuit, with raised decoration producing a comparable effect when lighted. One such piece, white glazed and in the form of a circular tower with encircling hunting scenes in relief, is in the Broulard Collection. A similar white-glazed pedestal in the Newman Collection has encircling relief decoration depicting two horse-drawn coaches in a woodland scene. Related to these is a circular tea warmer in the style of a church with dormer windows on the top of the pedestal and the cover of the teapot; made of translucent white biscuit, this piece, in the Blair Collection (Fig. 63), with counterparts in the Berthelot, Chiavassa, and Freed Collections, is not true lithophane.

All the above-described lithophane panels are white, as is normal. But there are two types of colored lithophane veilleuses. One has color impregnated into the body, so that it is white until illuminated, when it appears tinted; the other has a white body painted various colors. Two of the former type, in the Blair Collection, are, when lighted, dark sepia and green, respectively. Of the second type there are three in the Freed Collection: one, a conventional round tower with a beaded upper rim, has an encircling scene of houses, carriages, and figures, all polychrome; a second, in similar form, is painted dark green; and a third has a rectangular pedestal (like the white

Fig. 58. Paris. Gillet and Briançon patented lusterware, c. 1855-60. Freed Collection.

Fig. 59. Lithophane. Jacob Petit, 1830-50. Broulard Collection.

Fig. 60. Lithophane chapel. France. Broulard Collection.

Fig. 61. France. Lithophane rectangular. Baron A. de Tremblay, Rubelles, 1836-58. Newman Collection.

Fig. 62. France. Lithophane pentagonal. Blair Museum of
Lithophanes, Toledo, Ohio.

Fig. 63. France. Bisque church. Blair Museum of Lithophanes, Toledo, Ohio.

lithophane pieces described above) whose four panels have a painted dark blue ground dotted with gold stars and each a white intaglio bust.

Limoges has produced porcelain teapot veilleuses for over a hundred years. A fine Louis Philippe example, perhaps by the Limousin modeler, Etienne Baignol, has a pedestal in the form of a circular urn, with two handles, mounted on a drum base; on top of the urn rests the teapot. The decoration is small garlands and bands of gilt on a white ground.[130] A similarly shaped model, probably also from Limoges, but whose base has three claw feet, is in the Freed Collection; it is entirely gilded. (Fig. 64.) Both these pieces have encircling vent holes in the base and in the upper rim of the urn. A conventional circular tea warmer of white porcelain of Limoges, c. 1820, with gilt decoration, is in the Musée Adrien Dubouché, Limoges. Another such Limoges tea warmer, white with gold bands, bears the monogram of Honoré de Balzac.[131]

The Bayeux factory in Normandy, which started making hard-paste porcelain in 1793 at Valognes, made very fine tea warmers from 1812 to 1847 after it moved to Bayeux, and it continued to make pieces of good quality and originality until the end of the century. The early tea warmers are smaller than the usual veilleuses and are naïvely decorated with simple chinoiserie figures and flowers in pastel shades of pink, blue, and green; five examples are in the Berthelot Collection and one is in the Newman Collection. Later models, of normal size, are gracefully modeled and are usually decorated with the dark blue characteristic of Bayeux, quite often with red and gilt added; some have polychrome garlands and chinoiserie, and an occasional one is of orange or other hue.

A Bayeux example of the late period type from the factory of Veuve Langlois, 1830-47, in the Jean le Jeune Collection at Octeville (Cherbourg), is of conventional circular shape, with decoration of typical blue and gilt.[132] In the Musée de Bayeux there is a piece from the same factory with medallions of flowers and figures in polychrome on a blue ground.[133] More unusual in form is a tea warmer having at the sides of its circular pedestal two handles of hanging tassels; one such piece, in the Newman Collection, is blue and gold with polychrome floral sprays (Fig. 65), and similar examples are in the Berthelot and Brosio Collections. A very ornate urn-like Bayeux veilleuse has a circular pedestal which tapers narrowly as it joins the plinth containing the *godet*.[134] There are 12 Bayeux tea warmers of the later period in the Berthelot Collection, and others are in the Broulard, Chiavassa, Freed, and Newman Collections.

At Valentine, near Toulouse, porcelain tea warmers of rather heavy body were decorated with large low-relief leaves colored dark blue and green. The blue is very similar to the characteristic Bayeux blue. Examples are in the Berthelot, Broulard, Freed, and Newman Collections.

A very eye-catching tea warmer is in the Correr Museum (Ca'Rezzonico), Venice. (Fig. 66.) The pedestal, of rectangular shape but with gracefully curved sides, rests on a low base on which sits the *godet* within the pedestal. The teapot has a spout in the form of a serpent's head. The whole piece is richly decorated with polychrome flowers and gilt. This piece (formerly attributed at the Ca'Rezzonico to Austrian make, but more likely of French or possibly Bohemian origin) is being reproduced in Paris today, and copies may be easily purchased in almost any hue. There are two such pieces in the Freed Collection whose catalogue attributes them to Sèvres. (See Chapter 8 for a Russian counterpart.)

Entirely different from all other tea warmers is one whose source of heat was, rather than the usual *godet*, a glass tube set within the thin cylindrical pedestal. The pedestal has on one side a curved handle; the other side has an opening to expose a section of the glass tube. This tube, with a notched slot fitted to the porcelain piece above, can be rotated so as to expose on one side a frosted surface (to reduce the light) and on the other side a complicated (and unsolved) device of figures apparently arranged for timing; it is marked "*Breveté s.g.d.g*" ("*sans la garantie du gouvernement*"), which indicates that the timing system was patented. On top of the pedestal is a small hollow porcelain stand on which the teapot rests. One such piece, complete with the glass container, is in the Newman Collection; it is entirely white with gilt bands and with pierced Greek crosses in the stand below the squat teapot. (Fig. 67.) A similar piece (without the glass) is in the Freed Collection; it has apple-green

Fig. 64. Limoges. Freed Collection.

Fig. 65. Bayeux. Newman Collection.

Fig. 66. Paris (?). Correr Museum (Ca'Rezzonico), Venice.

112

Fig. 67. "Timer." France. Newman Collection.

Fig. 68. France. Lantern with painting-on-glass panels.
Newman Collection.

Fig. 69. France. Ovoid. G. Aîné & Cie. Newman Collection.

Fig. 70. Paris. Directoire, 1795-99. Gandur Collection.

ground and is decorated with painted flowers and Greek crosses. The pedestal of such a piece is in the Musée des Hospices, Lyons.

The variety of shapes of tea warmers seems limitless. An unusual one is in the form of a Revolutionary square lantern with glass panels on three sides, painted with street scenes, and a handle on the fourth side; inside is a very low candle socket instead of a *godet*. (Fig. 68.) Another unusual tea warmer, impressed "G. Ainé et Cie.," is in the form of an egg-shaped urn, divided mid-

116

Fig. 71. France. Charles X period, 1824-30. Gandur Collection.

Fig. 72. Pitcher. Freed Collection.

Fig. 73. Pavillion. Freed Collection.

Fig. 74. Lunéville, France. Mark: O. Paque. Broulard Collection.

way so that the upper half is the teapot; one such piece, decorated with polychrome floral sprays, is in the Newman Collection (Fig. 69) and another, white and undecorated, is in the Berthelot Collection. A rare Directoire veilleuse, hexagonal in shape, has its teapot suspended within three corner columns. (Fig. 70.) A rococo model, c. 1824-30, has dog's-head masks on the base. (Fig. 71.) Another ornate type has a pedestal in the form of a vase embellished with large leaves and floral stems in relief; one such piece is further decorated with an applied floral spray in bisque, and another, very large, has on the front of the pedestal the figure of a young girl. (Plate VIII.) A rare model is in the form of an urn-shaped pitcher (Fig. 72), and another is in the shape of a pavillion with eight columns supporting a "fish-scale" roof (Fig. 73). In the Berthelot Collection there is a rococo tea warmer that is

119

Fig. 75. France (?). Newman Collection.

of white-glazed porcelain completely ornamented with many attached bisque flowers and sprays.

Only a few French teapot veilleuses are in museums as most of the nineteenth-century pieces are not distinguished in quality or decoration. Many are conventional circular tea warmers with white ground, although some are green, blue, or of other hue (there are six unusual pink ones in the Berthelot Collection). They often have merely simple floral decoration, but some have painted or transfer-printed scenic panels or encircling scenes. On the other hand, some (such as those described above) are of good quality and modeling, and are made with artistic decoration; these make valuable additions to private collections.[135] The Victoria and Albert Museum has a tower tea warmer marked "Flamen Fleury à Paris," of Rue Faubourg St.-Denis, Paris, 1803-35; the pedestal has an encircling painted rustic scene, an upper band of lilac (similar to the base), and a red beaded upper rim. There are some unimportant pieces in the Musées Royaux d'Art et d'Histoire, Brussels (one is *porcelaine de Paris* decorated with floral garlands and bands of rose Pompadour and gilt, and another of *porcelaine de Paris* is decorated with a polychrome landscape), and another in the Musée Lorrain, Nancy (Empire style, with gilt decoration on a white ground). In the Metropolitan Museum of Art, New York, there is only one veilleuse (on loan); it is a mediocre tea warmer, probably Directoire, with a circular tower pedestal with beaded upper rim and black transfer-printed scenes.

A variation from tea warmers is the veilleuse which substitutes for the teapot a covered cup (resting in a *bain-marie*), used for warm milk. An early example is a faïence piece from Lunéville, in Lorraine, late eighteenth century, in the Broulard Collection. (Fig. 74.) It has a cylindrical pedestal and two scroll handles, and the cup has a loop handle. The entire piece is decorated with a pattern of crude blue dots on a white ground. The pedestal bears the mark of a shield surmounted by a royal crown, indicating that it was made by the Manufacture Royale Keller et Cuny; it also bears the name "O. Paque."

These cup veilleuses were made in France (and some in Italy) throughout the nineteenth century, usually of porcelain of good quality. One, in the Newman Collection, of unusual shape with a circular pedestal standing on three feet, is decorated with wide horizontal bands of dark green and black (Fig. 75); a similar piece in the Broulard Collection has the bands of irridescent straw color. A Bayeux example, in the Broulard Collection, is colored ochre and black and is decorated with Chinese-style birds and flowers. A faïence cup warmer, marked "Creil et Montereau," in the Broulard Collection is unusual in that the pedestal is wide like the food warmer pedestals and has two shell-shaped handles; it has an amusing scenic decoration showing a girl in a large crinoline ascending as if she were a basket balloon. There are other examples of cup warmers in the Berthelot, Broulard, Brosio, and Newman Collections.

# 5. Germany

Many leading German potteries which made household ware from 1755 to 1775 made food warmers of porcelain (Nymphenburg, Höchst, Frankenthal, and Fulda) and of faïence (Durlach, Hannoversch-Münden, Stralsund, Kelsterbach, and others). Tea warmer veilleuses were seldom made in Germany. There are, however, some large German kettles and coffeepots which, resting on a pedestal containing a *godet*, function in a similar manner. (See Chapter 17.)

Porcelain food warmers, called *Réchauds,* were a "specialty" of Nymphenburg, as a number of ceramic authorities have commented.[136] "These date from 1760 and preserve the rococo feeling."[137] They "were often superbly painted"[138]; "a rare collector's item."[139] The pedestals of the Nymphenburg *Réchauds* were made in four styles: (a) with straight but slightly sloping sides, (b) with slightly incurved (waisted) sides, (c) bell-shaped, and (d) square with chamfered corners and rococo decoration. The first three, which in the factory catalogue of 1755 were called *"Oefferlen sambt aller Zuegehör"*[140] (little stoves with their accessories), have on the pedestals two hooded vents (one over the aperture and one on the reverse) and two tassel-shaped handles. The bowl has a protruding flange which rests on the rim of the pedestal and has two lateral handles; some bowls show a rim rising about 1 inch above the flange. The dome-shaped cover has an ornamental finial, often a pear or twisted knob. The decoration is painted in enamel colors and usually represents outdoor scenes (frequently a romantic landscape or a Japanese garden with a per-gola, occasionally a medieval harbor scene with castle, boats, and figures) or, less often, floral sprays; in addition, there is lattice-work, scattered flowers, and insects.

Of the first type of Nymphenburg *Réchaud,* with straight sides, many examples are known. A handsome one, c. 1760-65, in the Kocher Collection at the Historisches Museum, Berne, Switzerland,[141] has on the pedestal, bowl, and cover encircling harbor landscapes painted by G. C. Lindemann, who seems to have specialized in decorating *Réchauds*. Above the aperture and just below the hooded vent is a coat of arms such as is occasionally seen on these pieces; this one is the coat of arms of Bavaria. (Fig. 76.) The piece is exceptional in that the rim of the bowl above the flange also is painted with an encircling landscape. A very similar piece, c. 1758, also painted by Lindemann with an encircling harbor scene, with ruins, ships, and figures, is in the collection of the Staatliche Porzellan-Manufaktur Nymphenburg, near Munich; it also has the Bavarian coat of arms and rich gilt decoration.

Two similarly modeled food warmers are in the Bayerisches National Museum, Munich; one, c. 1760, is decorated by Lindemann with an encircling landscape of a Japanese garden with a pergola,[142] and the other has rustic scenes (painter unknown). Slightly different is the Nymphenburg *Réchaud* in the Art Institute of Chicago, as its bowl has no decorated visible rim; its decoration, painted by Lindemann, is an encircling landscape on the pedestal and the cover.[143] Other such pieces, c. 1760, with garden and pergola scenes, are one in the Kunst-

122

Fig. 76. Nymphenburg, c. 1760-70. Kocher Collection, Historisches Museum, Berne.

Fig. 77. Nymphenburg, c. 1760-70. Kunstgewerbemuseum, Cologne.

gewerbemuseum, Cologne, Germany,[144] (Fig. 77) and one in the collection of José M. Mayorga, Havana.[145] The pedestal of a Nymphenburg *Réchaud* in the Victoria and Albert Museum, London, is decorated merely with polychrome birds and flowers, and is not of the same high quality as the others mentioned.[146] A food warmer of this type (lacking the cover) was offered for sale in New York City in 1964; its decoration is an encircling river scene with houses, figures, and a tombstone bearing the date 1759, and embellishments of polychrome floral sprays.

Some Nymphenburg *Réchauds* of this type, while made in the same 1755-65 period, were decorated at a later date. One, at the Staatliche Porzellan-Manufaktur Nymphenburg, has black and red arches and floral decoration, painted c. 1830-35; another in the same collection, decorated about the beginning of the nineteenth century, has only gold stripes and designs. A similar piece, in the Grossherzoglichen Privatsammlung, Prinz-Georg-Palais, Darmstadt, Germany, modeled c. 1765, was probably decorated c. 1830; the pedestal and cover have a pink ground, and the only decoration is black horizontal bands near the edges of each part and a black rococo pattern on the hoods and handles.

Also in the factory collection are three other pieces in this same form. One is decorated with large flowers, and one is without any painting. The third, c. 1765, decorated with a well-painted floral bouquet, is about 3 inches smaller than all the other pieces.

The Nymphenburg *Réchaud* with incurved (waisted) sides is exemplified by a piece, c. 1760, in the Museum für angewandte Kunst, Vienna, complete with matching *godet*. (Fig. 78.) The pedestal is decorated with a landscape of a Japanese garden with a pergola and fountains. Two such pieces, comparably decorated with a Japanese garden and pergola,[147] are privately owned in Munich, but have been on loan at the Bayerische National Museum, Munich.

A bell-shaped Nymphenburg *Réchaud*, in the Museum für Kunst und Gewerbe, Hamburg, Germany, has the characteristic two tassel-shaped handles, two hooded vents, and a twisted knob finial; it is decorated with a painting, predominantly in green, of a medieval harbor scene, with a castle, boats, and figures, and with polychrome flowers on the cover.[148] (Fig. 79.) Another bell-shaped food warmer, c. 1760-70, decorated with a land-scape of a castle and trees painted in blue (perhaps the only piece of Nymphenburg porcelain decorated in this color[149]) is in the same museum, as well as a similarly shaped pedestal, 1760-70, with a landscape painted in purple.[150]

The fourth type of Nymphenburg food warmer was introduced in the 1764 factory catalogue as "*bossierte. Aufwärm-ofen*"[151] (embossed rococo. *Réchauds*). It has a square rococo pedestal with chamfered corners, four rococo scroll feet (unlike the foot rim on the other Nymphenburg pedestals), two scroll handles (instead of the usual two tassel handles), and vertical slits for ventilation (instead of hooded vents). The bowl conforms to the contour and style of the pedestal and has two scroll handles. Its high-domed cover is surmounted by a phoenix rising from yellow and crimson-tipped flames. Such a piece, with a brown phoenix (restored at the Nymphenburg factory), is in the Stadtarchiv, Rosenheim, Germany.[152] (Plate XIII.) It is decorated with flame-like scrolls picked out in pastel shades of blue, pink, and green and also a polychrome floral garland on each side and on the reverse of the pedestal. Its *godet* is a small semi-globular painted cup that bears the underglaze blue hexagram mark of 1763-65. Local tradition in Rosenheim has it that this *Réchaud* was decorated by Franz Anton Bustelli, but it is not in his style and moreover, as he died in 1763, it seems unlikely that he did it in the last year of his life.

Another Nymphenburg *Réchaud* of this same rococo form (but lacking the *godet*) was sold in the 1961 auction of the Otto Blohm Collection, of Hamburg[153]; it has a gray phoenix and is decorated with flame-like scrolls picked out in blue, puce, green, brown, and gilt, as well as polychrome garlands on three sides of the pedestal. The pedestal, cover, and *godet* (conforming to the shape and style of the pedestal, and bearing the hexagram mark) of a third Nymphenburg food warmer of this type (lacking the bowl) is in the collection of the Staatliche Porzellan-Manufaktur Nymphenburg, Munich, where it and all the *Réchauds* of this rococo type are considered to have been modeled in 1763 by Johann Häringer who was paid by the factory in 1763 for making certain models; this piece is a part of a Häringer group that includes a candlestick, an inkstand, and a holy-water vase, all in rich rococo style. The pedestal and bowl of a fourth such

Fig. 78. Nymphenburg, c. 1760. Museum für angewandte
Kunst, Vienna.

126

Fig. 79. Nymphenburg, c. 1760-70. Museum für Kunst und
Gewerbe, Hamburg.

127

piece, but without the domed cover for the bowl, is in the Bayerische National Museum, Munich; it is decorated with pastel blue and pink flames, and it too has a covered *godet* conforming to the shape and decoration of the pedestal.[154] A similar pedestal (without the bowl, cover, and *godet*) is in the Museum des Kunsthandwerks (Grassi Museum), Leipzig, East Germany; it is white glazed with no painting.[155]

Höchst porcelain food warmers, c. 1755-70, often decorated with the characteristic red-violet enamel coloring, are very similar to the first type of *Réchaud* from Nymphenburg, except that the pedestals are slightly narrower and have two handles usually in the form of sharply modeled polychrome satyr-head masks. These mask handles are sometimes placed normally on each side of the aperture, but on some Höchst pedestals the masks are above the aperture and on the reverse, with the hooded air vents correspondingly transposed to the sides. The air vents are sometimes covered with conventional pointed hoods and occasionally covered by projecting scroll-like green leaves. The bowls have lateral handles and low-domed covers, with a fruit or artichoke finial.

A complete Höchst *Réchaud*, with mark, in the National Museum, Stockholm, has the usual polychrome masks over the aperture and on the reverse, and its decoration is a polychrome landscape with red-violet embellishments. (Fig. 80.) Another such Höchst food warmer, c. 1770, belongs to the Historical Museum, Frankfurt, but now is on loan at the Museum für Kunsthandwerk, Frankfurt[156]; its decoration is figures *en camaïeu* (red-violet) and small polychrome flowers, its air vents are green projecting scroll-like palm leaves (instead of the usual pointed hoods), its masks are the customary polychrome satyr-heads, and its finial is a green artichoke. A similar Höchst food warmer of this form (also with leaves over the vents) has been erroneously called a "*Brûle-Parfum*"[157]; it is decorated with four reserves of painted landscapes.

A complete example of a Höchst food warmer with the masks on the sides of the pedestal is in the Gandur Collection.[158] Another, lacking the cover, is in the Kunstgewerbemuseum, Cologne; its decoration is merely small polychrome floral sprays. In the Newman Collection there are two Höchst pedestals of this type; one, with underglaze blue wheel mark, is painted with a polychrome medieval river scene with castles and also butterflies and insects; the other, with underglaze iron-red wheel mark, is painted in polychrome with birds perched on branches.[159] A similarly modeled complete Höchst *Réchaud*, but white glazed and completely undecorated, is in the Museum für Kunsthandwerk, Frankfurt.

Three other Höchst *Réchauds*, privately owned in Frankfurt, all have the usual masks and hooded vents; one, complete, c. 1765, with the masks over the aperture and on the reverse, is decorated with painted figures, butterflies, and insects[160]; another, pedestal (*unterteil*) only, c. 1775, with the masks on the sides, has an elaborate polychrome landscape of waterfalls, castles, ruins, and figures[161]; and the third, pedestal only, c. 1775, has a polychrome landscape and flowers.[162] Two more Höchst food warmers are in the Musée Adrien Dubouché, Limoges, France; one is decorated with small figures and flowers, and the other with a scene of a doe on a hillock.[162-A] A Höchst food warmer, c. 1775, also in the Historical Museum, Frankfurt, differs from all the foregoing models in that on the sides of the pedestal are two shell-shaped handles (instead of masks) and the whole piece is taller than the others; it is decorated with floral sprays *en camaïeu* (red-violet) and the cover has a polychrome apple finial.[163]

A Frankenthal porcelain *Réchaud*, the pedestal of which tapers more than the Höchst pedestals, is in the Altertumsverein, Frankenthal; the pedestal and the bowl (lacking the cover) are decorated with floral sprays.[164] Another similarly modeled Frankenthal pedestal and bowl, in the Musées Royaux, Brussels, also has polychrome floral sprays.[165] (Fig. 81.) Both these pedestals, from the second half of the eighteenth century, have mask handles almost identically like the naturally colored satyr-head masks on the Höchst food warmer pedestals, but without the shell-like headdresses and ornamental collars of the Höchst pieces.

Fulda also made porcelain *Réchauds*, which were modeled in the form of the Höchst food warmers. The pedestals are cylindrical with slightly sloping sides, two mask handles, and two sharply-pointed hooded vents. One such piece, 1765-70, in the Museum für Kunst und Gewerbe, Hamburg, has satyr-head masks like the Höchst pedestals; it is decorated with polychrome pastoral landscapes on the front and reverse.[166] However, two other

Fig. 80. Höchst, c. 1770. National Museum, Stockholm.

Fig. 81. Frankenthal, c. 1770. Musées Royaux d'Art et
d'Histoire, Brussels.

Fulda food warmers have a different type of mask, not known on *Réchauds* from any other factory; they are large open-mouth beetle-browed male heads with a gray beard and a tuft of gray hair. One of these, c. 1770, in the Hessisches Landesmuseum, Kassel, Germany, is decorated with neo-classical painted floral swags.[167] The pedestal of another such piece, in the Newman Collection, has polychrome floral sprays. (Fig. 82.) These two pieces both bear the Fulda mark on the base in underglaze blue.

Faïence food warmers were also made in Germany. Several from Durlach, 1760-1775, are decorated in characteristic style of this factory, with painted figures of Chinese laborers. The pedestals, cylindrical with slightly sloping sides, have two shell-shaped handles and two hooded vents, and the bowls have two lateral shell handles and a domed cover. There is an example of this type in the Haus zum Kirschgarten, Historisches Museum, Basel.[168] (Fig. 83.) The pedestal of another, enameled in

130

Fig. 82. Fulda, c. 1760. Newman Collection.

Fig. 83. Durlach, 1760-65. Haus zum Kirschgarten, Historisches Museum, Basel.

132

blue and black, is in the Kurpfälzisches Museum, Heidelberg.[169] In the Badisches Landesmuseum, Karlsruhe, are three Durlach food warmers: one, complete, is decorated with chinoiserie in green and black[170]; another, lacking the cover, also has green and black Chinese figures[171]; and the third (complete, even with the *godet*), although similarly modeled, is white glazed without decoration. Quite different is a pedestal, c. 1760, attributed to Durlach, in the Bavarian National Museum, Munich; it is unusually wide and conical in shape, with no shell handles, but four hooded vents, and its decoration is polychrome floral sprays.

Also in the Badisches Landesmuseum, Karlsruhe, are two faïence food warmers of unknown provenance. One such piece, lacking the bowl, has a pedestal (with the mark "DC") of unique shape, being cylindrical as to its lower half and then tapering slightly inward; its rococo decoration is also unique, having relief scrollwork around the aperture, two large shell handles, and no air vents. It is painted, in red, purple, and green, with a diaper pattern and two pair of bantam roosters; between the two roosters on each side there is in relief a fleur-de-lys. The cover has a pear finial. The other piece, formerly considered from Durlach, has the Durlach form (it lacks the cover) and is decorated with floral bouquets.

A Hannoversch-Münden faïence food warmer pedestal, formerly in the Blohm Collection, is rounded toward the base and has long protruding handles in the form of animal-head masks, as well as two hooded vents; its floral decoration is painted in various enamel colors, rare for this factory.[172] Two other *Réchauds* from the second half of the eighteenth century (signed with the triple crescent mark), of the same ware, form, and decoration, are in the Heimatmuseum, Hannoversch-Münden, Germany; these have high overhanging covers that completely conceal the warming bowl.[173] (Fig. 84.)

At Stralsund, in Swedish Pomerania (East Germany today), faïence food warmers were made from 1757 to 1770, of which two specimens are in the Kulturhistorisches Museum, Stralsund, and three others destroyed in World War II are recorded in photographs there. All are of identical and unique conoidal or sugarloaf shape, with an oval aperture, two masks as pedestal handles, no handles on the warming bowl, and a high dome-shaped cover decorated with a finial in the form of an artichoke

with two relief leaves. The masks are Slavic male heads, with long pointed beards, elongated satyr ears, and protruding shell-shaped headdresses; openings in the eyes and mouth constitute the air vents. The two existing pieces have on the pedestal and on the cover a decoration of polychrome floral sprays on a white ground; one is in fine condition (Figs. 85a and 85b), but the other is badly damaged and much repaired. The three lost pieces were white glazed and undecorated.

The potteries at Kelsterbach (Hesse-Darmstadt) also made faïence food warmers in the eighteenth century. One complete piece and two pedestals are in the Prinz-Georg-Palais, Darmstadt. The cylindrical pedestals all have large pentagonal apertures, two tassel-hooded vents, and two large boldly modeled lion's-head handles. The complete *Réchaud* is stoneware with a cream-colored glaze (Fig. 86); the pedestals without a bowl are white-glazed earthenware, one undecorated and the other painted with a few floral sprays. All three bear the underglaze mark "HD" in manganese red.

A cream-colored undecorated *Réchaud* from Hanau, marked "HN," belonged to the Historical Museum, Frankfurt,[174] but the *Réchaud* was destroyed in World War II. Cylindrical in form with vertical sides, the pedestal had two tassel-hooded vents and, above the pentagonal aperture, a lion's-head mask; the bowl had two lateral flat handles and a low cover with a knob finial. This piece was almost identical with the complete *Réchaud* from Kelsterbach.

Some German factories made food warmers of cream-colored glazed earthenware in imitation of Wedgwood Queen's Ware. There are three such pieces in the Historical Museum, Basel. All have loop handles on the pedestals, rather like the Wedgwood pieces already described. One of these is tall, with a candle holder on the gadroon-edged cover and a mask and wings over the aperture. (Fig. 87.) The second is more like the German *Réchauds* in form, and is only 8 inches high. The third is very unusual: shaped like an urn, its sides curve down and inward to a very narrow plinth and its bowl has a high-domed cover; its decoration is tiny pierced Greek crosses in a diamond pattern and a shock-headed male mask. (Fig. 88.) This last one has the impressed mark of Zell (Baden), which is known to have made glazed earthenware from 1818 in the English style.[175]

Fig. 84. Hannoversch-Münden, c. 1770-80. Heimatmuseum,
Münden.

134

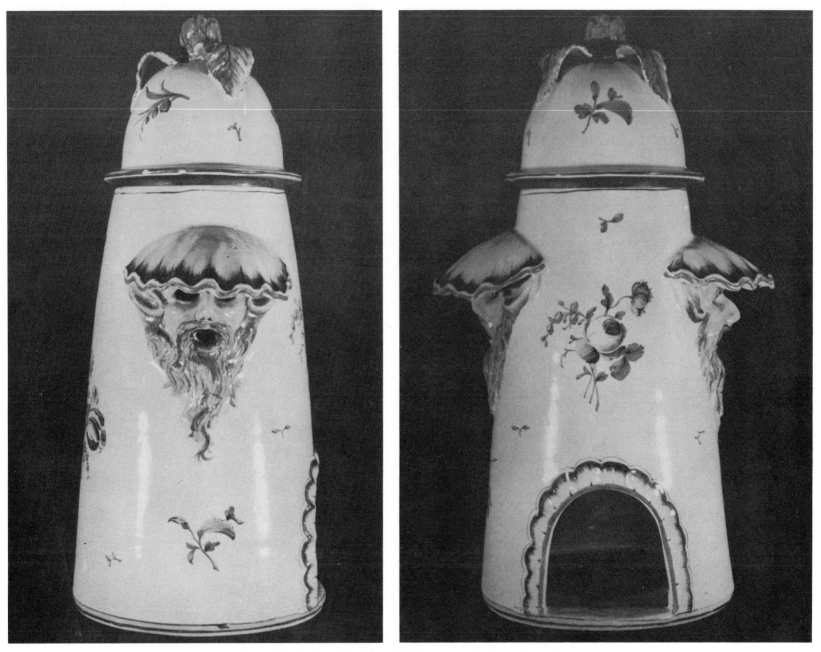

Fig. 85. Stralsund, ex-Swedish Pomerania (now East Germany), 1757-70. Kulturhistorisches Museum, Stralsund.

Fig. 86. Kelsterbach (Hesse-Darmstadt). Late eighteenth century. Mark: HD. Prinz-Georg-Palais, Darmstadt.

Fig. 87. Germany (?). Creamware. Historisches Museum, Basel.

136

Fig. 88. Germany (?). Creamware. Historisches Museum, Basel.

137

138

Fig. 89. Zell (Baden). Creamware. Newman Collection.

They are all from the late eighteenth century, as they are known to have been owned by Basel families at that time. A creamware teapot veilleuse, in the Newman Collection, is one of the few German tea warmers; it has an unusual aperture, a high teapot with an angular handle, unique mask handles, and a *godet* impressed "Zell." (Fig. 89.)

As noted above, few German veilleuses were made in the form of tea warmers. However, two Meissen pedestals have been seen that were made into lamps and whose shape, with aperture for a *godet*, indicated that they may have been pedestals for tea warmers, as they were too narrow for the usual warming bowl; they were decorated with multi-color applied flowers on a white ground. Also, the C. Tielsch & Co. factory at Altwasser, Silesia, with the mark "C.T.," made conventional tea warmers after 1845; they are not uncommon and are usually somewhat rococo with painted floral decoration.

Since 1872 veilleuses have been made by the factory of Carl Thieme, at Pottschappel, Dresden, known to have been a copyist. A *Réchaud* made there and bearing the factory's underglaze blue mark imitates (but in a slightly larger size) the typical Höchst models with the satyr-head mask handles on the pedestal and a pear finial on the cover. The pedestal and cover of one such model (examples are in the Chiavassa and Newman Collections) are decorated with large-scale polychrome floral bouquets, and the masks are unattractively picked out in burnt-orange color. This factory also made, at a later period, veilleuses of the type having a covered cup resting in a *bain-marie*; one such piece, in the Newman Collection, has mask handles (a ram's head) such as are usual on German food warmers but have not been seen elsewhere on a cup or teapot veilleuse, and its decoration consists of numerous narrow vertical gilt stripes overlaid with a polychrome floral pattern.

# 6. Italy

The many known Italian veilleuses are almost all of the teapot type, made after 1800 of glazed earthenware or of porcelain. There also are a few very fine Italian food warmers, most of which are of maiolica, from the second half of the eighteenth century.

A white tin-glazed maiolica piece, called a "food warmer," at the Museo "Duca di Martina," in the Villa Floridiana, Naples, has been traditionally attributed in Naples to "*maioliche di Capodimonte*" but it is now considered there, with more justification, to be probably from the Fabbrica Pasquale Rubati, Milan, late eighteenth century. (Fig. 90.) The baluster-shaped pedestal is somewhat squared with chamfered corners; at the top of each corner is a lion's-head mask with long mane and at the foot a lion's paw. The oval aperture is relatively small. The cover has two uplifted lateral handles and a flower-and-leaf finial. Inside there is a metal tray 4 inches deep, probably for charcoal. This fact and the large size of the piece, 20 inches high and 10 inches wide, suggest that it may not have been a food warmer (it lacks a bowl) but rather a foot warmer for floor use; several comparable pieces made in Belgium and so used are discussed in Chapter 17, and there is a strong possibility that this piece in Naples also came from Belgium or northern France.

A maiolica food warmer of unique form, made in the late eighteenth century, belongs to the Museo Civico Correr, Venice, and is in the Ca'Rezzonico, Venice (Fig. 91.) Formerly attributed to the Fabbrica Roberti "Fiera" of Treviso,[176] it is now believed, at the Correr Museum, to have been made at the Fabbrica Pasquale Antonibon, at Nove, near Bassano, Italy. Its modeling and decoration are very much in the style of Antonibon. The pedestal curiously consists of two parts: resting on the lower section is a conforming cylindrically shaped section that supports the two-handled and covered warming bowl. All the sections are fluted and curved, with polychrome floral decoration. This piece is unusual also in that it is a food warmer with no aperture to insert the *godet*, which rests within the lower section of the pedestal.

The Ginori factory at Doccia is said to have made one model of a food warmer in porcelain during its first period, 1737-57, and also others thereafter. No example from the first period is known, but one ascribed, on the basis of its decoration and colors, to Ginori's second period, 1758-91, belongs to the private R. S. Collection, Rome.[177] (Fig. 92.) The pedestal, with ornate hooded vents, wide aperture, relief floral swags, and low-relief masks under the scroll handles, is baluster shaped. The bowl rises about ½ inch above the flange that rests on the pedestal, and its cover has a low candle socket. The painted decoration on the pedestal and the cover is an encircling landscape. There is a similarly decorated circular *godet* with a lateral handle. A similar piece, but all white, is in the collection of Marchese Leonardo Ginori-Lisci, Florence, Italy, and another is in the collection of Avv. Alberto Robiati, Milan; a similarly

141

Fig. 90. Italy. Fabbrica Pasquale Rubati, Milan (?). Late
eighteenth century. Museo "Duca di Martina" (Villa Floridiana), Naples.

Fig. 91. Nove, Bassano. Fabbrica Pasquale Antonibon. Late eighteenth century. Correr Museum (Ca' Rezzonico), Venice.

142

Fig. 92. Doccia. Ginori, 1758-91. Collection of R. S., Rome.

143

Fig. 93. Pesaro. Casali and Calegari, 1770-80. Museo Civico, Turin.

shaped maiolica pedestal, less ornately decorated, is in the Museo Internazionale delle Ceramiche, Faenza. The form and the modeling of these pieces should be compared with those of the glazed earthenware pieces shown in Fig. 3 and Fig. 18.

A food warmer modeled differently from the usual English and Continental food warmers is a maiolica one from Pesaro (Casalis and Calegari factory), c. 1770-80, in the Victoria and Albert Museum, London.[178] The tall cylindrical pedestal has two handles in the form of grotesque masks below projecting shells, and it is decorated with painted Chinese figures and flowers. The pedestal and domed cover have encircling pierced work picked out in pink, as well as decoration in vivid colors and gilt. The base for the hollow pedestal is missing, but there is a bowl suspended within the pedestal by a flange. This piece is very similar in form and decoration to a Pesaro piece in the Museo Civico, Turin (Fig. 93), which, with other similar Italian pieces, all called perfume burners, is described in Chapter 17; the factors establishing this one as a food warmer are the bowl (which the others lack) and also the mask handles covering the vents as is customary on food warmers.

Closely related is a rare maiolica food warmer, in the collection of Dott. Francesco Liverani, Faenza, made by Conti Ferniani, Faenza, in the second half of the eighteenth century.[179] Its cylindrical pedestal, about half the height of the Pesaro pedestal described above, has two foliated loop handles, very similar to the three above-mentioned perfume burners. Resting on the pedestal is a cylindrical bowl, making the complete piece similar in height and appearance to the Pesaro food warmer (except that the handles are lower, on the bottom section, rather than midway on the tall pedestal of the Pesaro piece). The bowl has a domed cover with a mushroom finial, but it has no pierced work (as has the pedestal), which establishes that it is a food warmer rather than another perfume burner. The decoration of the bowl is a polychrome encircling landscape of Oriental inspiration with a "Casotto" motif. The lower section has encircling pierced work mingled with painted floral decoration in yellow, red, and blue; its foliated loop handles are dark green. The lower rim of this section and of the domed cover are orange. Another maiolica piece in identical form (but lacking the cover) is in the Museo Civico,

Bologna; also from Faenza, c. 1760, its decoration of polychrome Oriental landscape, floral motifs, and pierced work is very similar to that of the Ferniani food warmer at Faenza. A third piece, identically modeled but of uncertain provenance, is in the Newman Collection. (Fig. 94.) Its decoration, entirely in underglaze blue, is unusually interesting: on the bowl is the episcopal coat of arms of a Catholic bishop for whom the piece was presumably made, showing the tasseled hat and the emblem of clasped hands; on the top of the base, inside the pedestal, is the painted dial of a clock; and on the bottom of the bowl is an underglaze blue 16-pointed rosette. The decoration of this third piece is somewhat in the style used on Turin maiolica in the fashion of 'blue and white Moustiers ware from 1730 to 1745. That style, however, is too early for a piece in this form, and attribution to Turin seems unjustified. Although monochrome blue was rarely used at Faenza, attribution to a factory there or nearby seems more warranted in view of the close similarity to the two Faenza examples.

The pedestal only of a maiolica veilleuse from the Fabbrica Antonio Ferretti, of Lodi (near Milan), c. 1765, in the collection of Avv. Alberto Robiati, Milan,[180] was probably part of a food warmer rather than a tea warmer. (Fig. 95.) It is baluster shaped, with two rococo scroll handles. There are no hooded vents, but rather four tiny air holes near the upper rim. The decoration is a floral spray in pale green and pink, and around the top of the aperture is a rococo flame-like ornamentation in relief. The relief work is picked out in purple of Cassius. Although unmarked, it has many characteristics of the Ferretti factory at Lodi and it was certainly made there.

There must be considered in connection with this Lodi pedestal a faïence pedestal, formerly in a private collection at Zurich, that some years ago was attributed to the Johann Jacob Frey factory at Lenzburg, Switzerland.[181] This attribution seems to have been based mainly on the monogram mark $\mathcal{A}$ which was stated to have been that of Andreas Frey, brother or nephew of the owners of the Lenzburg factory. But the monogram is identical with that on various Antonio Ferretti pieces in the Museo Civico at Lodi (one of which is also marked "Lodi 1766"); the fact is that this monogram has been recognized by Lodi authorities as the Ferretti mark.[182] It is a coincidence that the initials of Andreas Frey and

**Fig. 94. Faenza (?). Newman Collection.**

Antonio Ferretti are the same, but it seems beyond the bounds of probability that two persons would adapt them into the same unusual monogram. Largely for this reason the Lodi authorities have recently attributed the pedestal in Zurich to Lodi.[183] But even more persuasive is a comparison of the Zurich pedestal with the Robiati pedestal; they are identical as to form, rococo handles, aperture shape, relief border, and foot rim, and the decoration on both is a polychrome floral bouquet in the style of other Ferretti work (comparable to the large-scale floral bouquets of Strasbourg). These similarities confirm the present attribution of the Zurich pedestal to Ferretti of Lodi rather than to Frey of Lenzburg.

A cream-colored glazed earthenware food warmer from the Fabbrica Fontebasso, Treviso, is in the Museo Civico Luigi Bailo, Treviso, Italy. Its cylindrical pedestal

Fig. 95. Lodi. Fabbrica Antonio Ferretti, c. 1780. Collection
of Dott. Alberto Robiati, Milan, Italy.

Fig. 96. Faenza, late eighteenth century. Museo Internazionale delle Ceramiche, Faenza.

148

has a pointed aperture, two double twisted rope handles, and a small pierced design. Its pot has a smooth loop handle, suggesting that the pot and its cover are not the original parts for the pedestal.

The pedestal and cover (lacking the bowl) of a maiolica food warmer from Faenza is in the Museo Internazionale delle Ceramiche, at Faenza, Italy. (Fig. 96.) The pedestal, with its vertical sides, very low and wide aperture, and absence of handles or masks, is similar to one later mentioned from South Tirol in Austria. The decoration at the top of the pedestal and around the edge of the cover is a formal polychrome floral pattern of garlands; at the bottom of the pedestal and on the angular hoods over the air vents are painted oak leaves. A piece of identical form (also lacking the bowl) and very similar decoration, in the Drake Collection, Toronto, is of unknown origin.

Coming now to Italian tea warmers, a very early one, possibly antedating 1800, has been attributed to Jacques Borelly (Giacomo Borelli), an Italian who made faïence at Marseilles and after 1779 at Savona, Italy. (Fig. 97.) It is in the Chiavassa Collection, Milan. Its maiolica pedestal and teapot are basically of conventional form but they have much ornate modeling. The decoration is blue and orange colored flowers and green leaves on an ivory ground. Two small handles on the pedestal are blue.

An oversize maiolica tea warmer believed to have been made by the Fabbrica Pasquale Antonibon, at Nove, near Bassano, Italy, 1774-1825, is in the Newman Collection. (Fig. 98.) It has an especially wide pedestal that rises vertically and then tapers inward so that its lines flow into those of the teapot. The entire piece has fluted modeling, in the usual style of Antonibon, and the grayish-white glaze is decorated with polychrome flowers predominantly in the characteristic muted shades of green, ocher, and blue. On the pedestal there are two handles of lion's-head masks concealing tiny air vents.

Another early tea warmer, possibly antedating 1800, is a handsome one, privately owned, from Pesaro, near Urbino. (Fig. 99.) It is of white-glazed maiolica with polychrome floral decoration. The pedestal has two tall angular loop handles, and the teapot has a most unusual angular kettle-type overhead handle.

A Pistoia tea warmer, c. 1790-1810, in the Brosio Collection, Museo Civico, Turin, is of glazed brown earthenware, and consists of a tall pedestal, a *bain-marie* (*bagnomaria*), and a pot with a cover.[184] (Fig. 100.) The whole piece is bullet-shaped. The circular pedestal has two small loop handles and its sole decoration is two rococo female masks. The pot has a similar loop handle, and its spout is modeled with a mask to conform to the pedestal.

Another Pistoia tea warmer, c. 1830, is in the Chiavassa Collection. (Fig. 101.) Its circular low pedestal and teapot, of marbled brown-glazed maiolica, are decorated with encircling bands of an arched pattern (pierced on the pedestal). The pot has a high curved handle and an animalistic spout.

A rustic tea warmer of sepia-glazed *terra cotta*, whose rough and pocked surface shows grains of grit in the clay, is probably from southern Italy. The wide circular pedestal tapers inward toward the bottom (which has no foot rim) and has a large aperture; it has no holes whatsoever as air vents. Both the pedestal and the pot have medallions of figures primitively molded in white slip. The form and decoration of this piece suggest that it dates from the transitional period about 1800 when tea warmers were first being made. One such piece is in the Newman Collection. (Fig. 102.) Three similar ones are in the Chiavassa Collection, Milan, and one is in the Freed Collection.

Three cylindrical tea warmers of creamware from the Fabbrica Fontebasso, Treviso, which imitated English creamware in the nineteenth century, are at the Museo Civico, Treviso. All are extravagantly decorated with encircling pierced work and depart radically from the English creamware models. One with loop handles on the pedestal has large pierced floral sprays. The pedestals of the other two have lion's-head masks, circular beaded bands near the bottom and the top, and pentagonal doors for the aperture (a feature seen elsewhere only on the food warmer from Nevers, France, described above); the pierced work includes a center medallion above the aperture with large openings and floral sprays. The teapot of one of these pieces has concave sides and its cover has a rose finial (Fig. 103); the other teapot is convex and has a knob finial.[185] All these Treviso pieces (as well as the Treviso food warmer described above) show the influence of English creamware models.

Two cylindrical *terraglia* tea warmers from Este were

150        Fig. 97. Savona, Jacques Borelly. Chiavassa Collection, Milan.

Fig. 98. Nove, Bassano. Fabbrica Pasquale Antonibon, 1774-1825. Newman Collection.

Fig. 99. Pesaro, late eighteenth century. Private Collection.

Fig. 100. Pistoia. Brosio Collection, Museo Civico, Turin.

Fig. 101. Pistoia. c. 1830. Chiavassa Collection, Milan.

154

Fig. 102. Italy, c. 1790-1810. Newman Collection.

Fig. 103. Treviso. Fabbrica Fontebasso. Museo Civico, Treviso.

156

shown in the Exhibit of Este Ceramics, at Este, Italy, in 1960.[186] Both are cream-colored, with pierced floral decoration. One, in the collection of Sig. Mario Marenesi, Este, is similar in shape to the Wedgwood tea warmers with loop handles; it is probably from the Fabbrica Girolamo Franchini, Este, which is known to have made tea warmers in cream-colored glazed earthenware.[187] The other, more ornate, has handles in the form of Pan, and the teapot has a spout in the form of the head of a griffin; it is in the collection of Dr. Ersilio Casarotti, Badia Tolesine, Italy. Another Este creamware tea warmer, in the Newman Collection, also is shaped very similar to the Wedgwood tea warmers, except that its two handles are shell-shaped, and it has on the front and the reverse pierced decoration in a modified version of the Wedgwood pattern; it bears the rare underglaze impressed mark "FG" for Girolamo Franchini.

A cream-colored glazed earthenware tea warmer, formerly attributed to the Fabbrica Fontebasso, Treviso, but now considered as probably from Este, is at the Correr Museum (Ca'Rezzonico), Venice.[188] Closely imitating the Wedgwood tea warmers in form and decoration, its cylindrical pedestal has an adaptation of the Wedgwood pierced leafage pattern. The pedestal and the teapot have double twisted rope handles attached by floral terminals, and the cover has a pear finial. The spout has an unusual horizontal opening. Another such pedestal, attributed to Treviso but perhaps also from Este, is at the Correr Museum.

There are two creamware tea warmers in the Brosio Collection at the Museo Civico, Turin, that Sig. Brosio has attributed to Rome, although without indicating any particular factory. One of these (Fig. 104) has much in common with the pieces from Treviso and Este, and it is believed that its origin in one of those places is more likely than in Rome. The elaborate pierced work on the pedestal will be recognized as an enlarged imitation of the Wedgwood pierced leafage spray, and the piercing is in the style of pieces from Este, while the small beaded band around the bottom of the pedestal is seen on pieces from Treviso. The handles, with the molded flowers within the loop, are unique. The other tea warmer attributed to Rome, c. 1790, has a conventional cylindrical pedestal with two loop handles and four small pierced-work groups; its ungainly teapot, which is unique, has

both an overhead kettle handle and, adjoining it, a small loop handle, and the spout is a very short cylindrical stump.

A creamware tea warmer from Trieste, made by Giuseppe Sinibaldi and Ludovico Santini, with their incised mark "SS" and so late eighteenth century, is in the Civici Musei di Storia ed Arte, Trieste.[189] It is in general in the form of the Wedgwood tea warmers, but the differences are significant. The pierced leafage pattern on the cylindrical pedestal is slightly different from the conventional Wedgwood design, but more revealing are the ornate handles on the pedestal in the form of negro-head masks under a projecting shell and the mermaid handle on the pot. The pedestal of another such piece, also incised "SS" and in the Trieste museum, has slightly different pierced decoration and the handles are satyr-head masks. A creamware tea warmer in the Museum für angewandte Kunst, Vienna, that combines features from these two Trieste pieces has long been questionably attributed by that museum to Leeds. (Fig. 105.) Its only difference from the first Trieste piece is that the handles on its pedestal are satyr-head masks with elongated ears and long pointed beards (like the second Trieste piece); the similarities indicate that it almost certainly came from the same Trieste factory.

Creamware tea warmers were also made at the Fabbrica Cecchetto-Baccin, at Nove, near Bassano, c. 1786-1810. Three known examples are in the shape of the Wedgwood tea warmers, but are larger in diameter (6 inches rather than Wedgwood's usual 5 inches). The pedestals have similar loop handles, but the terminals at the bottom have small male masks (comparable to the mask terminals on a Leeds teapot in the Donald C. Towner Collection and on some Cockpit Hill creamware teapots). The aperture is pointed and the pierced work (front and reverse) is a variation of the Wedgwood leafage design. The pot has a wide flange, like those from nearby Treviso. The *godet* has a cover with two holes, one for a wick (passing through a metal holder) and one for air. Two such pieces, both complete, have been in the family of the present owner, Rav. Antonio Cecchetto, Nove, for over 150 years. One has a double leafage pierced design (Fig. 106), the other a single spray. The third such piece, formerly in the same collection, is now in the Newman Collection.

Fig. 104. Italy. Treviso or Este. Brosio Collection, Museo
Civico, Turin.

Fig. 105. Trieste. Late eighteenth century. Fabbrica Giuseppe Sinibaldi e Ludovico Santini. Museum für angewandte Kunst, Vienna.

160  Fig. 106. Nove, Bassano. Fabbrica Cecchetto-Baccin, 1786-1810. Collection of Rag. Antonio Cecchetto, Nove.

Fig. 107. Italy (?). Creamware with indigo-blue masks, swags, and medallions. Newman Collection.

Fig. 108. Doccia. Ginori. Collection of Marchese Leonardo
Ginori-Lisci, Florence.

162

The pedestal only of a creamware veilleuse of unusual form and unique decoration, probably Italian, c. 1800, is in the Newman Collection. (Fig. 107.) The cylindrically shaped piece, whose body is somewhat thicker than the usual Italian or English creamware, has extensive pierced work in radiating patterns and around the gallery. There are four low-relief lion's-head masks connected by relief floral swags and also four relief floral medallions. The masks, swags, and medallions are in underglaze blue, as well as the formal hand-painted pattern around the bottom and the band inside the gallery. The masks and swags should be compared with those on the tea warmer (Fig. 16) attributed to Leeds (but possibly Italian) and on certain Wedgwood vases. A creamware tea warmer, complete, with very similar thick body and heavy glaze, is in the ceramic collection of Dott. Enrico Wallner, at the Hotel Due Torri, Verona, Italy; it is shaped like the typical Wedgwood tea warmers, but its loop handles are attached by leaf terminals (as on a tea warmer from Treviso) and the pierced leafage design on the pedestal is comparable to other Italian pierced work. The provenance of these two veilleuses is unknown, but it is believed that both are Italian, probably from Treviso.

A porcelain teapot veilleuse made by Luigi Tinelli, Milan, 1834-41, in the Tinelli private collection at Laveno, Italy, is of conventional shape, with polychrome floral sprays.[190] The only special feature is that the aperture is not the usual curved opening but a circular hole.

Many porcelain tea warmers were made by Ginori at Doccia in the mid-nineteenth century, generally of conventional form but with varying decoration. One oft-repeated model has a pyriform pedestal with three feet (above each of which are leaves in low relief) and a conforming pyriform teapot with a high-domed cover having a high pointed finial. (This model was also made in France, bearing the mark "H. A. & Cie.") One such

Ginori piece, in the Chiavassa Collection, has a black ground and is decorated, on the pedestal and the pot, with painted birds' nests containing three eggs and having a bird perched on each nest.[191] Another, in the collection of Marchese Ginori-Lisci, Florence, bears the words "*Buona Notte.*" (Fig. 108.) Other similarly modeled tea warmers are decorated with floral patterns or medallions of classical heads.

Two porcelain tea warmer veilleuses, in the Museo Internazionale delle Ceramiche at Faenza, Italy, are of uncertain but probably Italian provenance. One has an oval pedestal, on a separate base, decorated on its two sides with polychrome paintings bordered by simulated stonework; a similar piece is in the Newman Collection. The other is the pedestal of a circular tea warmer; it is decorated with an encircling colorful polychrome romantic scene.

Several other tea warmers of conventional shapes have been attributed to Italian origin in the mid-nineteenth century, such as a typical tower with beaded upper rim and encircling painted scene.[192] A red-orange tea warmer in the Chiavassa Collection, with medallions of classical heads, is said to be by Ginori, c. 1860.[193] Another, in the Brosio Collection, in the shape of a collapsible Chinese lantern and colored cyclamen, with conforming pot, is attributed to Naples, c. 1850[194]; a similar piece, colored light green, is in the Freed Collection, and one colored pink is in the Chiavassa Collection. An unusually shaped tea warmer in the Chiavassa Collection, attributed to Ginori, c. 1850, and said by Brosio to be in the style of Capodimonte, has a pedestal decorated on one side with relief satyrs and on the reverse with a donkey in relief, and its pitcher-shaped teapot has painted grape leaves and clusters[195]; three other such pieces are in the Chiavassa Collection, and three are in the Freed Collection (pitchers with the same relief figures are in the Ariana Museum, Geneva, and elsewhere).

Fig. 109. Vienna, 1780-90. Château des Rohan (Musée de Strasbourg), Strasbourg.

# 7. Austria

Austria produced a few food warmers of pottery and porcelain, as well as some porcelain tea warmers of fine translucent body.

A porcelain food warmer, c. 1780-90, bearing the Vienna beehive mark, is in the Château des Rohan, Strasbourg.[196] (Fig. 109). It is in the form of the Höchst *Réchauds*, with similar masks and hooded vents. The decoration of the entire piece is, in the style of Niderviller, *trompe l'oeil sur fond bois* in brown and white, with "attached" engraved pastoral landscapes on the pedestal and the cover *en camaïeu* (dark brown). The two satyr-head masks are entirely gilded.

Five peasant-type pottery food warmers are in the Museum für Volkskunde, Vienna. Two, from South Tirol, are glazed earthenware mottled dark green; the pedestals have shell-shaped hooded vents but no handles. One of these, c. 1780, is complete and is in the form of the typical Nymphenburg food warmer with straight sides except that it has an aperture so low that it is difficult to imagine the shape and size of the *godet* that could be inserted; it should be considered with the Faenza food warmer (Fig. 96) previously mentioned and the similar one of unknown source in the Drake Collection. The other South Tirol piece, perhaps early nineteenth century, is somewhat bell-shaped (it has a curious metal *godet*). The most unusual of this group, from South Tirol (Puster and Tauferer Tal), is made of very heavy body with dark brown glaze, and is cylindrical and rather tall; it has two angular handles and a deep close-fitting cylindrical bowl (the cover is missing). The other two are more conventional: one, possibly from Moravia or Lower Austria, is of creamware with sloping sides and shell-shaped handles; the other, with impressed mark "Neumark" and possibly from Pilsen, in Bohemia, is also of creamware with vertical sides and similar shell-shaped handles.

Several teapot veilleuses made of Vienna porcelain, bearing the beehive mark, are of characteristic form. Generally, the teapot is rather low and has a high perpendicular loop handle. The pedestal is usually in the form of a crenelated circular tower, often with a painted pattern of simulated stonework and with several holes as air vents. One such tea warmer, c. 1825, is in the Museum für angewandte Kunst, Vienna. (Fig. 110.) A similarly shaped piece, of Vienna porcelain with the beehive mark and the impressed date 1828, is in the Newman Collection; its pedestal is decorated with an encircling polychrome painting of a hunting scene with dogs chasing a stag. (Fig. 111.)

Fig. 110. Vienna, 1825. Museum für angewandte Kunst, Vienna.

167

Fig. 111. Vienna, 1828. Newman Collection.

# 8. Russia

Although no veilleuse made by the Imperial Porcelain Factory has come to light, several porcelain tea warmers from privately owned potteries, made in the first half of the nineteenth century, are known.

The factory of A. Popoff, at Gorbunovo, near Moscow, was founded in 1811. It made hard-paste porcelain and "its customers seem to have been mostly limited to the Russian court."[197] "The objects from this factory were of technical perfection, and of remarkable form and coloring . . . The painting of the porcelain left nothing to be desired."[198] From this factory came several known tea warmers bearing the mark "ΑΤ" in underglaze blue.

One Popoff model, 1830-40, of very translucent porcelain, is in the form of the conventional circular tower veilleuse with crenelated upper rim, but slightly taller than the French ones. The pedestal rests on a separate base decorated with painted simulated stonework. The significant feature is the decoration. The pedestal is exquisitely painted with an encircling landscape of hills, lakes, and medieval buildings, with several tiny figures of farmers and fishermen; the distant hills are painted lavender and above them the sky is unpainted semi-mat white. The teapot has a deep projecting bottom and the portion suspended within the pedestal is decorated with a classic pattern in gilt; the upper part of the pot is painted with a conforming encircling scene, and its cover has a similar painting in circular perspective. The crenelated rim of the pedestal is white glaze with gilt edge, as is the circular *godet*. One such piece, in the Newman Collection, has the tiny figures on the pedestal and on the teapot painted in gilt silhouette, perhaps inspired by the *Goldchinesen* style developed at Meissen and Augsburg, c. 1820-30. (Plate XIV.) A second such piece, in the Freed Collection, has a slightly different landscape, and the tiny figures are in natural colors.[199] Another, 1830-50, in the same form but decorated only with an overall brick pattern of gilt lines on a white ground, is in the State Historical Museum, Moscow.[200] The pedestal of a fourth such piece is in the Hermitage Museum, Leningrad; its decoration is also merely lines of gilt making an overall brickwork pattern.

Also by Popoff and in the Hermitage Museum is a tea warmer (Fig. 112) significantly similar in form to the piece of unknown (probably French) provenance in Venice shown in Fig. 66. Its main divergencies in modeling are the scroll feet on the base, the knob finial on the cover, and the handle on the teapot. The rococo decoration on the pedestal features applied floral sprays instead of the usual painted flowers.

Two other Popoff tea warmers, 1850-1872, are in the Museum at Moscow. Of oval shape, the pedestals of both are decorated with painted polychrome rural landscapes, together with much gilt and rich ornamentation.

The Miklashevski factory, at Volokitino, in the northeast Ukraine, also made porcelain tea warmers in the second quarter of the nineteenth century. One model, in the Hermitage Museum, has a pyriform pedestal on a separate base. (Fig. 113.) The pedestal has a high crown which, together with the modeling of the teapot, is very similar to the Jacob Petit model shown in Fig. 39. The

Fig. 112. Gorbunovo (Moscow). A. Popoff. Hermitage
Museum, Leningrad.

169

Fig. 113. Voloktino (Ukraine). A. Miklashevski. Hermitage Museum, Leningrad.

entire piece has a black ground decorated with much encrusted gilt, as well as white reserves on the pedestal and the pot with polychrome floral sprays.

Another Miklashevski model, in the Moscow Museum, is richly decorated with gilt on a cinnamon-brown ground. The pedestal has a polychrome painted scene with a shepherd and shepherdess tending their flock, and the teapot has white reserves with polychrome floral sprays.

# 9. Czechoslovakia

Bohemia was also a source of tea warmer veilleuses, although in very limited known quantity. One porcelain model is rather well represented in private collections today; the shape is standard but the coloring varies considerably. The very ornate one in the Newman Collection, with impressed Elbogen mark of a bent arm holding a sword, has a vase-shaped pedestal decorated with large leaves in relief at the top and sides of the pedestal; the conforming teapot has a leaf at the top. All the leaves have a white ground with blue veining and gilt trim. On the center of the pedestal and the pot are cartouches with polychrome floral sprays on a white ground. (Fig. 114.)

Another model of Bohemian tea warmer, c. 1830, has a pedestal in the form of the typical circular tower with crenelated upper rim, decorated with an encircling painted landscape of Karlovy-Vary (Karlsbad). The teapot has a high curved handle and an animalistic spout; it and the separate base are decorated in gilt with an encircling scroll. This piece, made at Pirkenhammer (Brezová), by Fischer and Reichenbach,[201] is in the Národní Galerie, Prague. (Fig. 115.)

A white-glazed earthenware food warmer made at Prague, c. 1800, is also at the Národní Galerie. It has the typical cylindrical pedestal, with a wide aperture, two shell-shaped handles, and two hooded vents; the high bowl has two lateral shell-shaped handles.

Fig. 114. Elbogen (Bohemia), Czechoslovakia. Newman Collection.

Fig. 115. Pirkenhammer (Brezová), Bohemia. Fischer and
Reichenbach, c. 1830. Národní Galerie, Prague.

# 10. Switzerland

Several Swiss potteries made food warmer veilleuses, most of which are of faïence. The only known Swiss tea-warmer veilleuses are of cream-colored glazed earthenware.

The Klug-Hünerwadel factory at Lenzburg made faïence *Réchauds* very similar in form to the German pieces, but a trifle smaller. One, complete with bowl and cover, made in the first period by Johann Jacob Frey, c. 1765 (mark "2 P/R"), has a pedestal with two tassel-hooded vents and with two handles in the form of male masks curiously extending no farther down than the mustached mouth; the decoration is sprays of flowers *en camaïeu* (dark brown).[202] A comparable piece, in the Ariana Museum, Geneva, has the same masks; similar hoods over the vents are decorated with vertical stripes of green, yellow, and blue, and the overall decoration is scattered polychrome leaves, flowers, and berries. Inside the pedestal the wreathing is more pronounced than on the English delft food warmers. A third such piece, in the Newman Collection, has similar masks and hoods, and the decoration is polychrome flowers and butterflies; the pedestal and cover are marked "A/Z" in light green.[203] (Plate XV.) Another pedestal attributed to this factory, c. 1767 (no mark), is of different form, having dog's-head masks, and is decorated with polychrome flowers, butterflies, and insects.[204]

A Lenzburg *Réchaud* from the same factory, 1762-67, in the Museum für Kunst und Gewerbe, Hamburg, Germany, has a similar cylindrical pedestal with two hooded vents and two dog's-head masks. (Fig. 116.) The pedestal is decorated with an enameled landscape of a mill with a waterwheel and figures, predominantly green and brown with red-brown borders; the cover has a similar rural scene. The unique feature is that, instead of the usual warming bowl, it has an invalid's cup with a drinking beak at the front. It was made by Markus Hünerwadel and decorated in the style of the painter Adam Heinrich Klug.

Also at Lenzburg was the factory of Johann Jacob Frey, 1775-96, and it too made faïence food warmers. One (without mark), attributed to this factory in its second period, is in the form of a German conical *Réchaud*, but it is made of brown-glazed earthenware.[205] Its pedestal has two tassel-hooded vents and two curious handles in the form of female masks with high feather headdresses. Its cover has a finial of fruit with two leaves.

A faïence food warmer pedestal, marked "$A$" in monogram, has been attributed to the same Frey factory at Lenzburg, and the initials have been said to be those of Andreas Frey.[206] The pedestal is baluster-shaped, with rococo scroll handles and an aperture having a molded border; its decoration is polychrome floral sprays. It is modeled and marked identically like the pedestal from the Fabbrica Antonio Ferretti, Lodi, Italy (Fig. 95) and, for the reasons heretofore stated in discussing that piece, it is now deemed to be from Lodi rather than Lenzburg.

Very different from all these are five faïence food

176      Fig. 116. Lenzburg (Klug-Hünerwadel). Johann Jacob
Frey, c. 1765. Museum für Kunst und Gewerbe, Hamburg.

Fig. 117. Bero-Münster (Lucerne), 1771-80. Schweizerische
Landesmuseum, Zurich.

Fig. 118. Zurich, c. 1775. Kirschgarten, Historisches Museum, Basel.

warmers from Bero-Münster (Lucerne), c. 1771-78, in the Schweizerische Landesmuseum, Zurich. They are most unusual in size, several being about 15 inches high and proportionately wider. One, complete, is bell-shaped and was decorated by Andreas Dolder, formerly employed at Niderviller; it has encrusted flower sprays and a polychrome coat of arms of Canon Ludwig Meyer v. Schauensee on whose estate at Bero-Münster Dolder's kiln stood.[207] (Fig. 117.) The other pieces are merely pedestals.[208] They are decorated with polychrome painted flowers, and two of them have sprays of encrusted flowers; the handles are in the form of tassels and the hoods over the vents are shell-shaped and picked out in crimson.

A Fribourg faïence food warmer (lacking the cover),

178

c. 1780, at the Ariana Museum, Geneva, is of conventional conical shape. The pedestal is decorated with polychrome floral sprays, and the two handles are masks resembling a dog's head. The bowl has two lateral handles.

A food warmer of Zurich porcelain, c. 1775, marked "Z" in blue, in the Kirschgarten of the Historisches Museum, Basel, is only 6 inches high, much smaller than usual veilleuses.[209] (Fig. 118.) The pedestal has two hooded vents and a uniquely shaped aperture. The bowl has a very wide flange and two lateral handles; its cover has a rose finial. The white ground is decorated with small polychrome flowers.

The Baylon factory at Carouge, near Geneva, made tea warmers of white *terre de pipe*, c. 1812. One marked piece, in the Newman Collection, has the identical shape as the Wedgwood tea warmers but is slightly smaller. The pierced leafage decoration over the aperture crudely imitates the Wedgwood pattern. A like piece is at the Ariana Museum, Geneva.

The potteries at Nyon, near Geneva, are known to have made faïence food warmers ("*veilleuses de malade*") and porcelain tea warmers ("*Réchauds à tisane*"),[210] as well as tea warmers of cream-colored glazed earthenware. The factory of J. A. Bonnard and Jean Jacques Robillard, near Nyon, made creamware in the style of Wedgwood, c. 1814-32. A tea warmer from this factory, in the form of the Wedgwood tea warmers, is at the Ariana Museum, Geneva. Its pedestal has interlaced strap handles of the usual loop shape and pierced work imitative of the Wedgwood leafage pattern. The bowl (with liner) has a small three-sectioned loop handle over its cover.

# 11. Belgium

There are relatively few known Belgian veilleuses. The pedestal of a faïence food warmer from the Fabrique de Péterinck, Tournai, 1751-99, is cylindrical, with two ram's-head masks above the aperture and on the reverse and with interlaced small loop handles.[211] The decoration is small sprays of flowers. It is part polychrome, part *en camaïeu* (rose-brown) on a white ground.

A porcelain food warmer from the Etterbeek pottery, Brussels, c. 1790-1803, is in the private collection of Mlle. A. Bara, Brussels.[212] Its cylindrical pedestal has two hooded vents and two shell handles; the pedestal and the bowl are decorated with flowers and floral garlands. What appears to be the base of a veilleuse, with the mark of this same factory, is in the Musées Royaux d'Art et d'Histoire, Brussels; made of white porcelain, it is in the form of an Ionic base resting on three feet and is decorated with gilt bands and with floral garlands in green and in rose-brown.

There are two porcelain tea warmers in this same museum, both attributed to Brussels. One, Louis Philippe period, has a typical crenelated tower pedestal (decorated with a polychrome painted scene of two children giving alms), a gilt base, and a gilt teapot. The other has a pedestal in the form of a tower with beaded upper rim and is decorated with a polychrome painted landscape.

A porcelain tea warmer from the Fabrique de Cappellemans, at Hal, Belgium, 1864-70, is in the Musée Communal de Bruxelles.[213] Its pedestal is in the form of a tower with beaded upper rim and rests on a separate base. The decoration is painted polychrome flowers on a black ground.

# 12. Luxembourg

A faïence food warmer from the Boch pottery at Septfontaines that started in 1767 is at the Musée des Arts Décoratifs, Paris. The cylindrical pedestal is of conventional form but slightly narrower than the usual French pieces; it has two lion's-head masks. The bowl has two flat lateral handles and a cover with a cherry and leaf finial. The entire piece has a white ground with decoration of cobalt blue horizontal bands and edges.

A tin-glazed food warmer of reddish-colored hard earthenware body, in the Newman Collection, is probably from Luxembourg. (Fig. 119.) It is of conventional food-warmer shape with slightly sloping sides and is complete with bowl, cover, and *godet*. The aperture of the pedestal is of unusual shape. The glazed ground is bluish white and the decoration is stylized floral sprays having horizontal leaves painted in cobalt blue. This decoration is identical with that on a goblet bearing the "BL" mark of the Boch pottery at Septfontaines, suggesting that this food warmer was also made or decorated there or, more likely, at the nearby pottery at Nimy. The style of decoration is that of Chantilly, which was copied in Luxembourg and northern France. On the bottom of the pedestal is the painted mark "Z/P." The whole piece has considerable "burst bubble" effect, perhaps due to refiring. Although the body and glaze are entirely different from Lenzburg pottery, it is curious that the shape, the hooded vents with vertical ribbing, the finial, the absence of a foot rim, and in general the aperture all resemble those of the Lenzburg pieces such as the one shown in Plate XV.

Fig. 119. Luxembourg. Nimy (?). Late eighteenth century.
Newman Collection.

# 13. Holland

Although many examples of English delft food warmers have been discussed, the only known veilleuse from Holland is not of Dutch delft but is a food warmer of porcelain of Weesp, c. 1760-70, at the National Museum of Wales, Cardiff.[213-A] Only the pedestal remains. It is cylindrical with slightly sloping sides, similar in shape to the food warmer from Frankenthal shown in Fig. 81, and has a pointed aperture. There are no handles or masks, but four vents covered by pointed hoods having rococo relief modeling. The body is of cream color and the glaze has a slightly brownish discoloration. The only decoration is a small spray of flowers painted in natural colors above the aperture. The factory mark on the bottom is in underglaze blue.

A curious faïence piece in the Musées Royaux, Brussels, formerly attributed to Flanders, is now considered to be from the Makkum pottery in Friesland, Holland. It appears to be the pedestal, only four inches high, of a veilleuse, octagonal in shape and with a large aperture for inserting the *godet*.[214] Accompanying it is a cup with a small loop handle; if this cup was meant to be the *godet*, it fits in the aperture only with difficulty; if it was to rest on the pedestal, the hole on the top of the pedestal is too large to support it, so that probably there was originally a supporting grille.[215]

# 14. Portugal

The Vista Alegre factory has been making porcelain tea warmers since its founding in 1824 to the present day. In its new museum at Ilhova, in northern Portugal, it has some interesting specimens of varied character.

The oldest is a tea warmer of white porcelain, c. 1824, with an oversized pedestal decorated with handles in the form of gargoyles; the sides of the teapot are somewhat concave. There is also a similar model without a teapot.

A very handsome teapot veilleuse, c. 1835, is in the private collection of the Pinto-Basto family, owners of Vista Alegre for generations. (Plate XVI.) Its round pedestal is divided by vertical gold framing into three large panels, each of which has, on a black ground, a painted scene of colorful Thai dancers encircled by polychrome garlands of flowers. The separate base (with four feet) and the top border of the pedestal are apple-green with thin white horizontal stripes, and the con-ventionally shaped teapot is *mat-brillant*, the ground of bright gold decorated with matted cherubs. The pedestal of this piece was painted by Victor François Chartier Rousseau, the French artist, who was the head decorator at Vista Alegre from 1835 to 1852.[216] There is a similar teapot in the Vista Alegre Museum of which the pedestal and base are missing.

Among the other pieces in this museum are tea warmers in the form of half-timbered round cottages, with a man's head peeking out of a gable window in the teapot; there is one entirely in white, 1850-60, and another in brown, c.1890. Also, there are Vista Alegre tea warmers with a square pedestal in lithophane. There is another in the form of a round cottage resting on a saucer, and there are seven pieces in conventional round form with polychrome floral decoration.

# 15. Spain

A tea warmer of faïence made at La Moncloa, Madrid, and signed by Daniel de Zuloaga Boneta, c. 1882, is in the Zuloaga Ceramic Exhibit, Segovia, Spain. (Fig. 120.) Although comparatively modern, it is interesting because it is the only known veilleuse made in Spain. The form is very similar to the Wedgwood tea warmers, with a wide cylindrical pedestal and with a globular teapot having a three-sectioned loop handle (the cover and the *godet* are missing). The pedestal has two unique griffin-mask handles and diamond-shaped pierced work on both sides. The entire piece has an ivory-white ground decorated in cobalt blue with floral sprays in the style of the Spanish Renaissance.

Fig. 120. La Moncloa, Spain. Daniel de Zuloaga Boneta, c. 1882. Zuloaga Ceramic Exhibit, Segovia.

# 16. United States

At least one American pottery, Tucker and Hemphill, of Philadelphia, which operated from 1825 to 1838, made veilleuses of the teapot type during its so-called third, or Hemphill, period, 1832-37. Soon after 1832 "artists and artisans were brought from France . . . The French forms were reproduced to a considerable extent. The body of the ware is extremely hard and of excellent quality, while the glaze is of superior character. The decorations are entirely hand-painted . . . always over the glaze, in brown or sepia monochrome."[217] "Some of the ware, sold at the present time for French work by ignorant bric-a-brac dealers, was made at Philadelphia between 1833 and 1838."[218]

In the Tucker Pattern Book, at the Philadelphia Museum of Art, two styles of tea warmers are shown: one has a pedestal in the form of the conventional crenelated tower (in two sizes); the other has an urn-shaped vase pedestal. None of the latter type is known to exist, but of the former type one was made, 1832-35, expressly for the Hemphill family by the best workmen of the factory and was at one time in the private collection of Mrs. Robert Coleman Hemphill; its pedestal has been described as "the *chef d'oeuvre* of this group . . . of thin, transparent porcelain, exquisitely decorated with a continuous rural scene in bright colors, extending around the center."[219]

Six Tucker and Hemphill tea warmers of the tower type were shown at the 1957 Tucker China Exhibit at the Philadelphia Art Museum.[220] Two complete pieces so exhibited (and two others without the teapot) are in the Philadelphia Museum of Art. One of these complete pieces, c. 1836, has as decoration on the teapot a painted scene *en camaïeu* (sepia) of the Schuykill Waterworks (the site of the pottery), at Fairmount, Pennsylvania, and on the pedestal a similarly painted pastoral scene with a farmhouse and figures.[221] The other complete piece has roses and a floral decoration on the teapot and the base and an encircling pastoral scene on the tower pedestal. Another of such exhibited pieces, in the Garvan Collection at Yale University, New Haven, Connecticut, has polychrome floral decorations and gilt. Two others, in private collections, have floral decoration on the teapots and bases, and on the pedestal romantic pastoral river scenes with figures. The sixth exhibited piece, also privately owned, has decoration in gold and claret. The air vents of some of these pedestals are star-shaped, of others circular; and of one at Philadelphia, the air vents are alternately circular and oblong.

Another Tucker tea warmer, of the same crenelated tower form, was in the Philip H. Hammerslough Collection of Tucker Ware, formerly exhibited at the Wadsworth Atheneum, Hartford, Connecticut. It is now owned by the William Penn Memorial Museum, Harrisburg, Pennsylvania. (Fig. 121.) Its tower pedestal has an encircling landscape showing a thatched half-timbered house, an arched stone bridge, and a castle with a tower. The base and teapot are decorated with roses and other flowers. All the decoration is painted over the glaze. The air vents of the pedestal are star-shaped, those of the base circular.

Fig. 121. Philadelphia, Pennsylvania. Tucker and Hemphill, 1832-37. William Penn Memorial Museum, Harrisburg, Pennsylvania.

188

Fig. 122. United States (?). Newman Collection.

There is a complete tea warmer in the Newman Collection that might be Tucker ware. It has on the crenelated tower pedestal an overglaze sepia painted eagle with spread wings and a ribbon inscribed "E Pluribus Unum"; its right claw grasps an olive branch and its left a sheaf of arrows (curiously, pointing inward). Below the eagle there is a ribbon inscribed "United States of America." (Fig. 122.) Although the very thin and translucent white porcelain is finer than usual Tucker ware and the spout and handle of the pot are not characteristically shaped, the sepia tones and the American motif suggest Tucker (an eagle in various attitudes has been painted on Tucker pieces), or possibly a Tucker artisan at some other nearby pottery.

# 17. Objects Related to the Veilleuse

There are several types of ceramic objects that are not veilleuses but that are related in appearance, purpose, or method of use. Some function like a veilleuse but differ in form (hot water kettles with stands, coffee makers with stands, warming urns); others are similar in appearance but their purpose is not to provide heat (perfume burners, figurine flacons, and tobacco jars); and still others provide heat to warm food (argylls, warming plates and bowls, plate warmers) but their appearance as well as method of use is different. Also, there are foot warmers, night lights, and nursery lamps that have some resemblance in appearance or method of operation. All being somehow related to veilleuses, a few specimens of each group will be mentioned here for comparison.

KETTLES WITH STANDS. Reference has been made to ceramic kettles that function like a veilleuse in that they heat water by means of a heating device placed in a stand below the kettle. As they are for use by day and by more than one person, they are not regarded as veilleuses. Another basic difference is that such kettles have a flat bottom rather than an elongated bottom like the teapots that project downward into the pedestal of a veilleuse. But these ceramic kettles with stands, similar to some silver kettles with stands (and in fact modeled like these silver precursors, especially those c. 1725-35 that had globular kettles), function like a veilleuse and were made by some of the same potteries and during the same period, 1760-80.[222]

Many such ceramic kettles with stands are known. They were made in practically all the countries that made ceramic veilleuses. From England there are specimens in Leeds creamware; one, in the City Art Gallery, Leeds, with a globular kettle on a basin-shaped stand that contains a copper receptacle for charcoal,[223] is similar in appearance and operation to the Japanese tea ceremony stoves and kettles mentioned in Chapter 2. Two other almost identical Leeds kettles and stands are privately owned,[224] and two such Leeds creamware stands (the kettles with them are not the matching originals) are at the Leeds City Art Gallery.[225] Another Leeds creamware piece, at the Victoria and Albert Museum, London, with a similar globular kettle but a waisted cylindrical stand, is painted and printed in black.[226] A kettle and basin-shaped stand of unglazed red stoneware, rose-engine-turned, also at the Victoria and Albert Museum, was formerly attributed to Wedgwood and is now labeled Staffordshire; its many features of modeling and pierced-work decoration identical with the Leeds creamware kettles and stands confirm its present recognition as Leeds.[227]

Continental examples usually have a globular kettle, and the stands hold a spirit lamp or a *godet* under the kettle. French ones are the Paris (Clignancourt), 1775-98, porcelain kettle and stand, white ground with gilt decoration, in the Victoria and Albert Museum,[228] and the two comparable Clignancourt pieces in the Musée Céramique de Rouen[229]; another Clignancourt model is in the Musée des Arts Décoratifs, Paris. From Germany are Meissen porcelain examples, c. 1770, that have globular kettles and three-legged rococo stands that contain a *godet*; such pieces, in the Floridiana Museum, Naples, Italy, in the Národní Galerie, Prague,[230] and formerly in the Schlossmuseum, Berlin,[231] are decorated with polychrome painted bouquets and attached flowers. There are similar German pieces from Berlin[232] and Fürstenberg.[233]

Several Dutch kettles with stands are of glazed earthenware. Early delftware pieces rest on basin-shaped stands similar to the Leeds models, such as the 1744 example in the Rijksmuseum, Amsterdam,[234] and a privately-owned 1745 model[235]; another is in the Musées Royaux d'Art et d'Histoire, Brussels,[236] and there is one of Arnhem faïence at the Arnhem Municipal Museum.[237] Later delftware models by Geertruy Verstelle, c. 1764, have globular kettles on tripod stands, both sections fluted and painted blue; examples are in the Victoria and Albert Museum,[238] the Rijksmuseum,[239] and the Musées Royaux, Brussels,[240] and a comparable model is in the Metropolitan Art Museum, New York.[241] A delftware basin-shaped stand with an *écuelle*, in the Musées Royaux, is the only known food warmer of this large type.[242]

A Zurich porcelain kettle and stand is in the Schweizerische Landesmuseum, Zurich,[243] and one of cream-colored glazed earthenware, made by the Baylon factory at Carouge, near Geneva, in imitation of Wedgwood but with horizontal brown stripes, is in the Ariana Museum, Geneva. There is a Chinese globular porcelain kettle with a metal stand, made for the export trade in the Ch'ien Lung period, c. 1760; the kettle is enameled in *famille rose* style.[244]

An unusual coffee warmer in the Newman Collection, of white porcelain with gold bands, bears an unidentified mark, an underglaze "T.P.M." in blue beneath a crown (possibly for P. Donath, Tiefenfurth, Silesia). The pyriform coffeepot, 9 inches high, stands on a wide pedestal only 3 inches high, but with the usual aperture (and *godet*) and three other conforming small openings. This piece has no coffee-making apparatus like the coffee-makers described below, but it is not a true veilleuse as the pot is flat-bottomed and too large for use by one person.

COFFEE MAKERS. Also closely related to the veilleuse is the coffee-making apparatus (coffeepot surmounted by a coffee dripper) that rests on a pedestal in which sits a *godet* to provide warming heat.

A typical utensil of this sort is a white-glazed undecorated percolator in the Wellcome Museum, London, probably of German provenance but unmarked. A comparatively low pedestal containing the *godet* supports a large globular coffeepot, with a handle and with a metal tip on the spout. A separate cylindrical piece, resting atop the pot, is to hold the coffee grounds and has small holes in its bottom as in a standard coffee dripper; beneath this and suspended within the pot is another cylindrical piece (also with small holes in its bottom) that has a metal cone through which the rising steam passes into the upper piece before it condenses and descends through the coffee grounds. A separate cover fits the coffeepot as well as the dripper when placed above the pot.

Somewhat similar in form and operation, but incomparably finer in quality, is a coffeepot, pedestal, *godet*, and dripper, made of Vienna porcelain (bearing the beehive mark in underglaze blue and the impressed date 1813) in the Newman Collection. The coffeepot sits on a wide cylindrical pedestal with a covered *godet* in the usual aperture. There is also, to be placed atop the pot, a tall baluster-shaped coffee dripper with a perforated bottom and a porcelain tamper to press down the coffee grounds. Accompanying it are a small pot for hot water, a milk pitcher, a covered sugar bowl, and five small cylindrical cups ("coffee cans") with saucers. All are decorated *en suite*[245] with a stylized pattern of leaves in gilt, purple, and dark green. There is in the Musées Royaux d'Art et d'Histoire, Brussels, a pedestal and coffeepot, with dripper and tamper, all of identical form in white porcelain with gilt bands. Bearing the mark, in red, of Jean Nast, Rue Popincourt, Paris, c. 1810-1835, this piece was possibly copied from the Vienna model, but was probably made in Vienna in white and decorated by Nast.

Quite different in form, but apparently operating similarly, is a piece called a "*Kaffeemaschine*" made at Schlaggenwald, in Bohemia, c. 1834. It is a tall, cylindrically shaped triple-decker, consisting of a low pedestal with a *godet*, a pot with a spout and handle, and above that another conforming pot that is a dripper with a handle and cover. The decoration is painted landscapes and gilt bands.[246]

Another coffee-maker, made in Berlin, 1837-44, and

marked "K.M.P.," has a cylindrical pot resting on a circular base in which sits the *godet*. The spout and overhead handle are of brass. This Biedemeier piece, in the Markisches Museum, Berlin, is decorated with polychrome flowers, leaves, and butterflies, as well as gilt bands.

WARMING URNS. Another "cousin" of the veilleuse is the rare, tall porcelain one-piece urn with a spigot, in which a liquid is heated by means of a burner in an aperture in the plinth below the urn. Although these pieces function in the same manner as the veilleuse, warming urns are wholly different in appearance and, like kettles on stands, serve more than one person. They are in the shape of a round hollow column, about 16 inches high. At the base of the column there is a hollow plinth, three sides of which are pierced for air circulation and the fourth side open to give access to the warming chamber. The column has a cover and, near its bottom, an outlet for a metal spigot.

One such urn is in the Victoria and Albert Museum. Called a "tea urn," it has been attributed to Swansea, 1815-22, but now it is considered to be French porcelain. The three closed sides of the plinth are pierced in the form of an openwork arcade of interlocking arches. It has polychrome floral decoration on a white ground. The spigot is missing. An urn of identical form, but made of Pontypool japan-tinned iron sheet, is in the National Museum of Wales.[247]

Another such porcelain urn, called a *"Kaffeemaschine,"* from Ludwigsburg, has a similar round column (complete with a metal spigot) and a pierced square plinth.[248] The decoration is simple gilt bands on a white ground. A similar urn of *porcelaine de Paris*, decorated in the style of *Retour d'Egypte*, is in a French private collection.[249]

Closely related in form and use is a Du Paquier porcelain urn from Vienna, c. 1725.[250] Called a *"Warmwasserbehälter aus einem Teeservice"* or a "hot-water urn of a tea-set," it is a tall, triangular, covered urn resting on a three-footed base and having a hole for a missing spigot; under the urn, a spirit lamp at one time rested on the base. The urn is ornately decorated with the figure of a mythological animal at each corner (the mouth of one held the spigot).

Another columnar porcelain vessel for holding liquid and presumably for keeping it warm, but without any provision for heating and without any base or spigot, was made by Du Paquier, c. 1735-44, in several very similar models. These consist of a tall square urn with recessed chamfered corners in which stand tiny figures; the domed cover is decorated to simulate the pierced work on the lower part of the urn. One such piece, in the Museo Civico, Turin, has been referred to as "purpose unknown."[251] Another, similarly modeled but with different figures, in the Irwin Untermyer Collection, New York City, has been described as a "Covered vessel . . . The interior fitted with a brass sieve and a (painted) porcelain lining."[252] It is this insulating lining that suggests a purpose to retain heat. A third such urn, with a zinc liner, has been called "A very rare Du Paquier Vienna Vase or perhaps a Food Warmer."[253] The pedestal of another such piece, without the cover, is in the Kunstgewerbemuseum, Cologne, Germany.

A porcelain coffee urn of Weesp, Holland, 1762-70, in the collection of Mr. Bernard Houthakker, Amsterdam, is pyriform shaped and has three tall legs within which sits the porcelain godet.[254] The pot has two large animal-head handles, a high domed cover, and a metal spigot protruding from a low-relief animal mask, and it is decorated with a polychrome landscape.

A very curious warming urn in the form of a steam locomotive is in the Shelburne Museum, Shelburne, Vermont.[255] The piece, c. 1830, consists of a locomotive on a metal chassis, with a porcelain boiler and smokestack, followed by a four-wheel metal tender and then another two-wheel metal car on which rests a small porcelain "fuel-box." The locomotive is 11½ inches long overall, and 13½ inches high to the top of the smokestack. The ceramic part of the locomotive is decorated with polychrome field flowers and wheat on a white ground, with gold bands. It bears the mark "Toselli Paris." At the front of the locomotive (whose boiler contains the liquid to be kept warm) there is a small spigot, and under the locomotive there is a holder for a small burner.

PERFUME BURNERS. Certainly a porcelain perfume or incense burner (*brûle-parfum*) is not in the food warmer family. However, some of these pieces function in the very same manner, with the perfume jar set above a pedestal in which is a burner. Despite their basic difference in form, the term "perfume burner" has, in at least two instances (referred to above[256]), been erroneously applied to a food warmer. It therefore seems relevant to call attention to a few specimens to emphasize the differences.

The typical *brûle-parfum* differs greatly from a food warmer. It is usually more ornate and airy; but essentially (1) there are openings in the cover for the incense fumes to escape; and (2) the flame under the perfume jar is often exposed, rather than enclosed within a pedestal as in the case of a food warmer (as required in the latter to provide the greater heat needed for food warming).

In the Victoria and Albert Museum there is a *brûle-parfum*, called a "pastille burner," of Höchst porcelain, 1780-85. A small urn for the flame is set inside a very open four-legged pedestal; another small urn for the incense rests on top. The complete piece is about 8 inches high. It is slate-blue and gilt, with a painted bust in gray on the perfume jar. The Prinz-Georg-Palais, Darmstadt, Germany, has another such Höchst piece, c. 1775, almost identical in form but of undecorated white glaze.[257]

Another so-called "pastille burner" in the Victoria and Albert Museum is of German porcelain, c. 1775, decorated at The Hague. It is smaller than those from Höchst, and its pedestal containing the burner has three legs which support the incense holder; the decoration is pink flowers and gilt on a white ground. A Nymphenburg "pastille burner," c. 1760-65, was in the Blohm Collection, Hamburg.[258] A Meissen perfume burner, c. 1750, has a *godet* resting on a small pedestal on which two cherubs stand supporting the perfume jar above the flame.[259] A Ludwigsburg piece, about 12 inches high, is ornately modeled with garlands in relief and rococo medallions, and is painted with colored birds.[260] Another comparably ornate specimen is of Berlin porcelain.[261] Somewhat different is an Italian perfume burner in the Museo Civico, Treviso, from the Fabbrica Antonibon, at Nove; it has a cylindrical pedestal, with pierced work, resting on a separate base and surmounted by a conical cover.[262]

The term "pastille burner" might be more properly confined to the piece that does not warm incense over a flame but that contains a smoldering perfumed pastille made of powdered charcoal and aromatic resin. Examples of these are the English castle and cottage pastille burners of bone china, c. 1810-60, whose only resemblance to a veilleuse is the aperture at the rear of the piece for inserting the pastille or the separation into two sections so that the pastille may be inserted.[263]

Three maiolica pieces, almost identical to each other in form but entirely different from those described above, are probably also perfume burners. They are modeled similarly to the Pesaro food warmer at the Victoria and Albert Museum, but do not have a warming bowl as that piece does. Each has a large cylindrical pedestal resting on a low circular waisted base and having two large foliated loop handles (instead of masks). Each has a high domed cover with a fruit finial. And each has elaborate encircling pierced work on the pedestal and the cover. They echo the Venetian bronze perfume burners described in Chapter 2. One, in the Museo Civico, Turin, Italy, and called a *"Bruciaprofumi,"* is made by Casali and Calegari, Pesaro, c. 1770-80; it is decorated with two polychrome scenic medallions.[264] (Fig. 93.) Another, in the Newman Collection, has the same form and pierced work, but is decorated, on the pedestal and cover, with black painted landscapes having polychrome floral surrounds; it bears on the base the word "Sceaux" in enamel blue, but it is believed to be not from Sceaux but more likely Italian and falsely marked, or possibly made by a later French provincial copyist. The third such piece, from the factory of Pasquale Antonibon, Nove, near Bassano, Italy, c. 1760, formerly in the Luciana Valcarenghi Collection, Milan, and also called a *"Bruciaprofumi,"* is similarly modeled, but the pierced work is less intricate than on the other two; its decoration is polychrome flowers.[265] Although such pieces closely resemble the Pesaro food warmer and also the Faenza food warmers of the type shown in Fig. 94, they lack bowls and the top of the base is slightly concave (so that a *godet* would not properly rest on it); these features support their classification by the Italian writers as perfume burners.

FIGURINE FLACONS AND TOBACCO JARS. Although wholly unrelated to veilleuses (as they are not intended to provide heat in any manner), these ceramic utensils in the form of figures are mentioned here because some are very similar in modeling and decoration to the *personnage* veilleuses, and upon first glance they are not readily distinguishable. In fact, often the identical figures of *personnage* veilleuses were made as ornamental figurines standing on a plinth,[266] and apparently the same model was sometimes used as a figurine, a *flacon*, and a veilleuse.

The *flacons*, used for wine or, smaller, for perfume, are undivided hollow figures which pour through an opening in the head (or occasionally an upraised arm). Perhaps having their origin in the Ralph Wood Bacchus jug, c. 1780, such figure-shaped flasks were popular later in England, c. 1830, usually of brown salt-glazed stoneware or earthenware. A white stoneware flask in the form of the young Queen Victoria, in the Victoria and Albert Museum, is inscribed "Lambeth 1837."[267] A *flacon à liqueur*, c. 1840, in the form of a Chinese mandarin figure, is from the factory of Veuve Langlois at Bayeux, France; the figure is colorfully attired in a green gown over which is a blue kimono with floral decoration and he holds a drinking cup.[268] Several French *flacons à parfum* are deceptively similar except for the ornate *bouchons*.[269]

Occasionally a one-piece tobacco jar with cover has been made from the same figurine mold that has been used also to make a *personnage* veilleuse. In the Freed Collection there is such a veilleuse in the form of a bust of St. Matthew (similar to Fig. P-87) and an identically modeled tobacco jar has been seen.

ARGYLLS. An argyll (or argyle), sometimes called a "gravy warmer," is a type of food warmer whose source of heat, unlike that of a veilleuse, is not a flame but hot water.[270] It is similar in shape to a covered coffeepot with a handle and a curved spout. The characteristic feature is that the gravy is kept warm by hot water that is poured into a separate compartment through an opening at its rear; this water compartment is created either by a lining wall or by a false bottom below which is the water. Thus it is functionally related to the Yung-chêng wine-pot described in Chapter 2. Although the argyll has been defined as a vessel "of silver or metal,"[271] several ceramic specimens are known.

One such piece, of Liverpool Delft, described as "an Argyle, with Container for Hot Water to keep Contents heated,"[272] has its loop handle and its spout on opposite sides of the pot, with a small opening by the top of the handle to receive the hot water; its cover projects over the opening, and the whole piece is decorated with a painted floral pattern. Other such pieces are known to have been made of English delft in the eighteenth century.[273] A rare argyll of Lambeth or Bristol delft, c. 1780-90, is in the Ashmolean Museum, Oxford, England.

A similar Wedgwood argyll is in the collection of the Old South Meeting House, Boston, Massachusetts.[274] It has been described as a "cream color argyle or gravy-warmer . . . labeled a 'Herb Steeper' . . . used for herb tea by Abigail Adams, wife of John Adams, second president of the United States."[275] It is stated that this argyll "named for the fifth Duke of Argyle . . . was an invention attributed to Wedgwood who pictures one in his catalogue of 1774."[276]

Another marked Wedgwood argyll, c. 1810, differs from the two mentioned above in that "the handle is at right angles to the spout as in the drawing in the 1774 Catalogue and the design is blue-printed and Oriental in character."[277] This piece had a projecting opening about midway down on the side opposite the spout, for pouring in the hot water. An engraving of such a piece, called "a gravy warmer," is shown in the early Wedgwood catalogues,[278] which describe these utensils as "Gravy Cups, with Water Pans." Two similar argylls (one of pearlware) are in the Buten Museum of Wedgwood, Merion, Pennsylvania,[279] and one is in the Wedgwood Museum, Barlaston, England.

A different type of Wedgwood argyll (no existing example is known) is shaped like an ordinary covered globular teapot with the hot water intake under the handle at the rear and opposite the spout.[280]

WARMING PLATES AND BOWLS. Another group of flameless ceramic food warmers consists of plates and bowls, of porcelain or pottery, with provision for keeping food warm by use of hot water or hot sand. Several of these ancestors of the veilleuse came from the Far East between the fifteenth and eighteenth centuries.

A Chinese warming plate, c. 1780, very similar in design and appearance to the baby's warming plate of today, is in the Victoria and Albert Museum. This 12-inch double plate has, at its edge, a projection with a hole for putting in the hot water. There are two small holes at the side of the projection which suggest that there was also a hinged cover. The decoration is polychrome flowers on a white ground.

In the British Museum, London, there is a pottery warming bowl from the Chia Ching period (1522-66). About 6 inches wide, it is shallow and has a double bottom. The base has a small hole in the center, presumably for pouring hot water or sand into the hollow space inside. A similar bowl, of *cloissonné* enamel of the same period, is in the collection of Mr. Soame Jenyns, London.

Another such warming bowl, somewhat deeper, is in the Victoria and Albert Museum. It is of Ming porcelain; perhaps from the fifteenth century, and is decorated with blue painted design in the linear style.[281] Another has been described as a "Ch'u-chou *yao* hot water bowl made with the shallow concavity at top and a hole in the bottom so that it can be filled with hot water to keep rice or other food warm."[282]

More recent examples of such hot-water warming plates are the one of Leeds creamware in the collection of Mr. Donald C. Towner, London, and the one of Liverpool delft sold in the collection of the late Prof. F. H. Garner.[283]

Still another flameless forbear of the veilleuse is a large plate, about 15 inches in diameter, with two close concentric ridges on the base; the resultant groove enabled the plate to fit snugly over the hollow stand that, presumably, contained hot sand. These were made in China in the mid-seventeenth century, in the transition period between the Ming and Ch'ing dynasties, for export to the Near East. One such plate (without the base), decorated in underglaze blue in bold design, is in the British Museum.

A different type of food-warming utensil that also used no flame consists of a covered soup tureen set atop another bowl for hot water. Within the lower bowl and below the tureen is suspended a smaller bowl for keeping warm a meat course. Such pieces, called *scaldavivande*, were made in Italy in the eighteenth century. Two, from the Fabbrica A. Ferretti, Lodi, c. 1760, are of maiolica with polychrome floral decoration; one is in the Museo Civico, Lodi,[284] and the other (lacking the inner bowl) is in the collection of Sig. Saul Levy, Milan.[285]

A related type of food warmer utensil, which also does not derive its heat from a flame, has been called a "food carrier." This consists of several similar shallow bowls stacked above each other so that hot water in the lowest bowl keeps warm the contents of the upper bowls. An example in Wedgwood undecorated creamware is in the Wedgwood Museum, Barlaston, England. One of maiolica from the Fabbrica Antonibon, Nove, near Bassano, Italy, late eighteenth century, in the Correr Museum (Ca'Rezzonico), Venice, consists of three identically shaped bowls, one above the other, forming a severe cylindrical piece; each bowl has a pair of similar plain projecting angular handles and polychrome floral decoration.[286]

PLATE WARMERS. Another member of the food warmer family is the low pedestal, with aperture for a *godet*, on which is placed a plate or platter to be kept warm. There is one of lusterware, marked "Sewell and Donkin," in the Drake Collection, rounded rectangular in shape, with two small scroll handles and a wide aperture; the handles and the rim of the aperture and of the top are outlined in copper luster, and the whole piece is decorated with marbled blue, mauve, green, and yellow.

Wedgwood made such a plate warmer of creamware[287] and also of jasper. Called a "Dutch stove" in the *First Shape Book*, it is a low circular pedestal with a wide rectangular aperture for the *godet* and decoration of encircling pierced work; the godet, rectangular with rounded bottom, is undecorated. A specimen of the jasper warmer, decorated with four figures in white relief, is in the Buten Museum. As the name implies, it was made to warm an unassociated flat-bottom plate. The dishes shown on the same page of the Wedgwood Catalogue obviously were not intended to fit on the ridge of the warmer.

FOOT WARMERS. It is the overall appearance of these ceramic objects, and especially the small oval aperture at the bottom, that leads one to think, especially from a photograph that does not indicate size, that they might be food warmers. The piece at Naples heretofore described (Fig. 90) is representative of this group. Although it has been called at Naples a "food warmer," it too may well be one of those braziers (*braseros*) or foot warmers (*chaufferettes*) which were common in Flanders and northern France. The charcoal fuel was probably inserted through the top into the metal brazier suspended inside, and the small aperture was probably merely to permit an air draft.

A piece almost identical with the one at Naples and also about 20 inches high is made of faïence, probably from Tournai, Belgium, or in any case Flanders or northern France, mid-eighteenth century.[288] Its baluster-shaped pedestal has the same corner ornamentation topped with lion's-head masks and manes and the same small oval aperture. Instead of being entirely white glazed, it has blue marbled decoration. It has a bowl with two scroll handles (suggesting that the piece in Naples perhaps had such a bowl originally) but lacks the cover (which the Italian piece has). A similar example is in the collection of M. René Desclée at Tournai.

Two comparable utensils are in the Musées Royaux d'Art et d'Histoire, Brussels. They are of similar form and size, with like aperture, but they have two side handles to facilitate carrying. Both are of undecorated white-glazed faïence of Brussels, late eighteenth century.

NIGHT LAMPS. As mentioned above, the earliest ancestor of the veilleuse was the simple oil night lamp frequently seen in collections of ancient pottery. But the nineteenth-century tendency to embellish ceramic ware reached this simple household utensil. One example, in the Newman Collection, is a tall porcelain piece with a pentagonal plinth surmounted by a conforming spire with painted stained-glass-window decoration on each panel; it has a lavender ground with dark green decoration. The flame from the bowl of the plinth gave illumination through the holes in the spire. (This piece may have been used as a pastille burner.)

TIN NURSERY LAMPS. There are a number of American-made warmers of japanned tin or tole ware, either undecorated or with stenciled floral designs in color, which function exactly like ceramic veilleuses. Several are in private collections.[289] Usually called "nursery lamps" or "milk warmers," they are tall and cylindrically shaped, with two hooded vents at the sides. Most have a warming bowl suspended by a flanged edge within the pedestal or within a *bain-marie* that hangs within the pedestal. All of these pieces have a hinged and latched door over the aperture for the godet, which is usually a small metal spirit lamp. Food warmers of this type are in the American Museum, Claverton Manor, Bath, England, in the Drake Collection, in the Lura Woodside Watkins Collection,[290] and in the Newman Collection. In the collection of Old Sturbridge Village, Massachusetts, there is an identical piece and also another very similar one; in addition, there is a japanned-tin warmer surmounted by a tin teapot, the whole a bit taller and thinner than the usual ceramic tea warmer.

A plebeian relative of the ceramic food warmer veilleuse was Samuel Clarke's "Pyramid" Nursery Lamp Food Warmer, made before 1867 in London and in Newark, New Jersey.[291] One of these popular and widely-advertised nineteenth-century warming utensils is at the Wellcome Museum, London, another is in the Drake Collection, and one is in the Watkins Collection.[292] The pedestal, of tin, is a cylindrical stand (with one loop handle) supported by three high legs that are attached to a circular base. Atop the pedestal rests a cylindrical tin receptacle (also with one loop handle) for hot water, and suspended in this receptacle by a flanged edge is a white porcelain patented pot ("pannikin"), with a special form of pouring lip and cover. The significant feature of these pieces is the source of heat, which is a "patented night light" rather than a *godet* for oil and wick; this light was a special stubby candle within a glass chimney, similar to that used in so-called "Fairy Lamps." The pot has inscribed on it the caution, "Clarke's patent 'Pyramid' Night Lights are the only Lights suitable for these Lamps," and on the opposite side is the amusing doggerel, "When nights are dark, then think of Clarke/Who's hit the mark precisely/ For his Night-Lights create Light Nights/ In which you see quite nicely." The porcelain cover bears further advice as to use, and also the trademark "Fairy", together with the notation "Reg. in U.S. Pat. Off." These were an improvement on the American tole-ware warmers in that the milk or other contents was heated in porcelain rather than in tin.

# 18. The Itinerant Influence

The present survey of a single ceramic object, the veilleuse, which was made contemporaneously in many countries, emphasizes the well-known fact that a particular model or style of decoration was often used at almost the same time by widely scattered potteries. This cross-section of ceramics, observed in a horizontal review as contrasted with the usual vertical treatises that cover one country or factory, focuses attention on the migratory habits of the artisans in those days, which fact of course affords a ready explanation of the often recurring similar features of veilleuses made hundreds of miles apart.

The most conspicuous and far-reaching example is the crenelated tower tea warmer. Specimens have been shown from England (Fig. 21), France (Fig. 38), Vienna (Figs. 110, 111), Bohemia (Fig. 115), and Russia (Plate XIV), and even as far as Philadelphia (Fig. 121). One would be hard pressed to say which was first, but surely those from Minton, Russia, and Philadelphia were the result of the French influence well known to have existed at the potteries there. The example from Portugal (Plate XVI), while an elaborate version of the tower, is of course due to the French background of Rousseau who had been brought to Vista Alegre by its founder.

Another very apparent example is found in noting the influence of Wedgwood's Queen's Ware, which extended to potteries in France, Germany, Italy, and Switzerland. Here a distinction must be made between the potteries that merely imitated the creamware and created their own models, and those that slavishly copied the Wedgwood conventional models with their characteristic pierced leafage pattern. Among the latter group may be cited the Baylon factory near Geneva, whose tea warmer differs only in quality of workmanship from the Wedgwood original (Fig. 7). Others who used, or adapted with only minor variations of detail, the pierced leafage design and applied it to similarly shaped models were the Trieste factory (Fig. 105) and Chamot & Cie., in France. On the other hand, there were some potteries that started from the Wedgwood model and attempted to create in creamware their own versions. Here the outstanding examples are found in Germany (such as the veilleuses of uncertain provenance shown in Figs. 87 and 88) and Italy (Fig. 105). The Italians let their enthusiasm carry them to extreme examples of pierced work in creamware models (such as those shown in Figs. 103 and 107) while still retaining the basic concepts of Wedgwood and Leeds.

An instance where distance was not so great is the English delftware food warmer (Fig. 1). The cylindrical glazed earthenware models, of which 33 have been mentioned above, show the same hand in the modeling and in the painted decoration, and it is only the differing body and glaze that leads to attributing some to Bristol, in western England, and others to Lambeth, in London. Even on the one known piece where the modeler departed from the norm by placing a scroll finial on the cover (as on the pedestals) instead of the usual candle socket, the painted decoration is like the others.

Another example of international influence is the food warmer with baluster-shaped pedestal that was made at

Lambeth (Fig. 3), in Staffordshire (Fig. 18), and also at Doccia in Italy (Fig. 92). The similarity of the shape, the relief floral garlands, the shell-like hoods over the air vents, the scroll handles, and the candle socket all point to a common ancestor . . . and the elaborate relief garlands suggest the original influence of a silversmith.

The polychrome floral bouquets painted by Joseph Hannong on the Niderviller food warmer (Fig. 24) and on the similar Niderviller pedestal in the Broulard Collection are very similar to those on the Frankenthal food warmer (Fig. 81) and attest to the short journey across the Rhine by Paul-Antoine Hannong, father of Joseph, when the enforcement of the Vincennes monopoly compelled him to leave France in 1755 to continue his work.

The satyr-head masks on the Frankenthal pedestal and the identical masks on most of the Höchst food warmers suggest some further traveling, a bare 45 miles. But the identical masks (although gilded) on the Vienna example (Fig. 109) indicate that someone made a longer journey; they were perhaps introduced by Johann Jacob Ringler who came from Vienna to Höchst in 1750.

Again, the identical lion's-head masks on the pedestals from Kelsterbach (Fig. 86) and from Hanau, as well as the great similarity of these pieces in general, reflect the short distance between these two potteries near Frankfurt. And the very similar lion's-head masks on the pedestal from the Rue Thiroux, Paris (Fig. 35), suggest again that someone traveled a bit farther.

Another case of resemblance is the Lenzburg faïence food warmer (Plate XV) and the one attributed to Boch or Nimy, in Luxembourg (Fig. 119). The overall similar shape, the absence of a foot rim, the button finials, and the rather unusual apertures all are points in common.

Even greater similarity exists between the large maiolica food (or foot) warmer attributed to Rubati, Milan (Fig. 90), and the foot warmer attributed to Tournai. Almost identical in shape and modeling, there seems certainly some relationship not yet established.

A baffling example is the ornate tea-warmer model that is being so often copied in Paris today. Whence came the original model? The piece in Venice (Fig. 66) is at least not of recent vintage, but whether it came from France or Bohemia (certainly not Vienna, as once considered in Venice) is uncertain. Many of the features suggest France, but the ornate details of decoration suggest Bohemian possibilities. In any case, the Popoff tea warmer (Fig. 112), of the same general shape and modeling, certainly establishes that its modeler had seen the other piece somewhere.

The French influence on Russian ceramists is attested by the Miklashevski tea warmer (Fig. 113) that so closely simulates the Jacob Petit model (Fig. 39).

The tall cylindrical piece that is debatably either a food warmer or a perfume burner is another example of similarity from different sources. The comparable pieces in Turin (Fig. 93) and at the Victoria and Albert Museum, respectively, are recognized as being from the same factory at Pesaro, Italy, but the one in the Newman Collection, with the enamel mark "Sceaux" and very closely similar in form and decoration, suggests an itinerant artisan. The example attributed to Antonibon, of Nove, near Bassano, Italy, shows much in common, as do the two Ferniani pieces from Faenza and the like piece shown in Fig. 94. Who influenced whom?

The many *personnages* raise similar questions. Most of them certainly were made in France, but did they influence the creation of other *personnages* elsewhere, such as in Italy? It may well be that some of the *personnages* were made outside France; for example, the colorful and oft-repeated Bacchus riding a goat (Fig. P–74) or Triton on a dolphin (Fig. P–75) might be from Naples, as has been suggested, but if so they were certainly influenced by Jacob Petit who made the Amphitrite riding a dolphin (Plate X and Fig. P–73) or by the other French veilleuses of other mythological persons riding dolphins (Figs. P–76 and P–77).

These instances suffice to establish the wide influence of many individual potters and decorators in various localities, to explain the recurring forms and styles of decoration of veilleuses made at places distantly separated, and to emphasize the difficulty, often the impossibility, of making definite attributions.

# 19. Cautions Concerning Veilleuses

The recent surge of interest in veilleuses, at a time when few good authentic specimens are available anywhere for purchase, makes it appropriate here (more so than in books on other types of ceramic ware) to add a few words of caution for unwary buyers of veilleuses.

Veilleuses of modern design are being made today in France, Italy, Portugal, and even in Japan. These are frankly sold as contemporary pieces by reputable shops. Many buyers seem to find them decorative as ornaments; they add nothing to a collection.

Many copies of old veilleuses (particularly tea warmers but also a few cup-warmer models) are being made in France today and, regrettably, all too often are offered by shops as antiques. Such pieces frequently bear a mark that is imitative of the Sèvres mark or that simulates some other authentic mark; occasionally some bear an original mark intended to suggest antiquity or the name of some decorator who never existed (or at least is unknown in any book on ceramics). These pieces may be bought, in many models and in a great variety of colors and decoration, from several wholesale porcelain dealers in and near the Rue Paradis, Paris, and from retail shops in Paris and throughout France, as well as in New York and elsewhere. A great many of these veilleuses find their way to the small provincial antique shops and to the stalls of the Paris Marché Suisse and Flea Market where many a tourist is duped by the contrived shabby environment. These reproductions are usually ornate and colorful pieces with much eye appeal (such as veilleuses of the type shown in Fig. 66). The unscrupulous dealers explain their occasional mint condition by some tale that they have remained untouched for generations in the cabinet of a relative. Some copies, on the other hand, simulate antiquity with scarred edges, rubbed gilt, accumulated dirt, and even a bit of soot on the bottom of the teapot.

The most insidious frauds are the "half-fakes." Here the imposter has recently purchased some undecorated white-glazed pieces (again usually tea warmers, but occasionally cup veilleuses) about one hundred years old which in their day were ordinary household ware or factory rejects, and now are purchasable throughout France at a nominal price; they have then been painted (and occasionally refired) to simulate the old designs and decoration. Thus, the fakers can, with half-honesty, say, "This is really an antique piece from about 1850" . . . but most of them change their tune when asked the date of the decoration.

Assembled pieces are all too often displayed by some dealers. These mismated veilleuses are pieces where one unit has been broken or lost, and a substitute has been provided from another broken veilleuse. The cover of the teapot may be of a different ware or with dissimilar gilding or decoration, even a poor fit or a wrong shape. The base under the pedestal may be a substitute that has no relationship to the rest of the piece except that it fits. Even the teapot itself may not be the original mate to the pedestal. Some such "marriages" are not detrimental (and in fact may be unrecognizable), as in the case of pieces made in quantity, such as Wedgwood creamware models, where originally the separate parts were mass produced and assembled, and so initially they were "married" rather than made as a unit.

On the other hand, it is fairly normal to find even the finest veilleuses without the original *godet*; although matching *godets* are obviously desirable, many veilleuses, even some in museums, lack this fragile part or merely have a simple ceramic substitute. In fact, a matching *godet* is so infrequent that one should be a warning of possible modern production.

Many veilleuses have, from frequent use or handling, been chipped or broken. While perfect specimens are of course preferable, it must be realized that usage for over one hundred years, and even much longer for the eighteenth-century food warmers, takes its toll. Small chips and even cracks are not calamitous, and in fact are preferable to crude restoration. Quite often today, veilleuses, especially tea warmers and *personnage*s, are offered for sale repaired, at times crudely but occasionally with such restoring skill as to defy ready detection. Examine each piece carefully and in a good light, preferably after cleaning it. Look particularly at the juncture of the handles and of the finial to detect off-white areas where lacquer has been applied to conceal a poor repair. Check the gilt portions to see if any part has a dull finish from cheaply-applied gilt paint (often easily rubbed off), quite unlike the original fired gilt; and note whether any gilt is rich old honey-gilt or later brassy mercuric gilt. On *personnages*, examine the protruding parts, such as hands, fans, etc., and particularly headdresses on the covers, to ascertain whether any broken bits have been replaced by plaster-like repair material which is unglazed but painted in some off-color hue and then lacquered (even extending a bit over the original glazed areas). Good restoration should not debar a worthy piece from a collection but any restoration must naturally affect the price.

# Album of Personnages<sup>*</sup>

Fig. P-1. Marquise holding teapot. Newman Collection.
A-1; C-2; F-1; N-1; T-1. Also Musée Céramique de Rouen.

* (See Note 10 for explanation of initials in captions.)

Fig. P-2. Marquise holding fan and rose, with a dog. Broulard Collection. A-2; B-1; C-5; F-3; G-2; N-2; T-2.

Fig. P-3. Marquise with a dog on lap. Broulard Collection. A-1; B-1; C-6; F-3; G-1; N-1; T-1.

Fig. P-4. Madame du Barry. Broulard Collection, A-1; B-1. (See Plate V.)

203

Fig. P-5. Court dwarf. Newman Collection. A-1; C-3; F-2;
G-1; N-1; T-1.

Fig. P-7. Queen holding dog at her shoulder. Georges Berthelot Collection. A-1.

204

Fig. P-6. Queen holding dog at her waist. Broulard Collection. A-1; B-1; C-2; F-3.

Fig. P-8. Elizabethan lady holding scroll. Freed Collection.
C-3; F-2; G-1.

Fig. P-9. Girl holding macaw. Freed Collection. F-1.

Fig. P-11. Girl, standing, holding fan. Broulard Collection.
B-1.

Fig. P-10. Girl, seated, holding fan. Brosio Collection, Museo Civico, Turin. C-1; F-2; T-1.

Fig. P-12. Girl pointing to hat. Gandur Collection. A-1;
G-1.

206

Fig. P-13. Girl holding bagpipe. Brosio Collection, Museo
Civico, Turin. A-1; C-3; F-2; T-3.

Fig. P-14. Girl playing mandolin. Broulard Collection B-1;
F-2.

Fig. P-15. Girl holding bird and letter. Freed Collection. C-1; F-1.

Fig. P-16. Girl holding bird. Gandur Collection. F-2; G-1; T-1.

Fig. P-17. Girl with dove on shoulder. Freed Collection. F-1.

Fig. P-18. Girl holding hair braid. Freed Collection. C-1; F-1.

209

Fig. P-19. Girl with crock on head. Chiavassa Collection, C-1.

Fig. P-20. Girl with teapot on head. Freed Collection. F-1.

210

Fig. P-21. Girl holding bobbin. Gandur Collection. A-1; C-2; F-1; G-1; T-2.

Fig. P-22. Girl saluting. Freeed Collection. F-2; T-1.

Fig. P-24. Girl holding goblet and grapes. Newman Collection. G-1; N-1.

Fig. P-23. Girl holding basket and jar. Freed Collection. A-1; B-1; C-3; F-2; N-2. (See Fig. 40.)

212

Fig. P-25. Girl holding basket and grapes. Chiavassa Collection. C-1.

Fig. P-27. Fortune teller seated by a sundial, holding a letter. Broulard Collection. B-1; C-1; F-2; T-1.

Fig. P-26. La Vivandière holding cask. Brosio Collection, Museo Civico, Turin. C-1; F-1; T-1.

Fig. P-28. Gardener. Gandur Collection. G-1.

Fig. P-30. Spanish dancing girl. Gandur Collection. C-3; F-2; G-1.

Fig. P-29. Gardener's wife holding sprinkler. Freed Collection. A-1; C-1; F-1; G-1.

214

Fig. P-31. Musketeer with dog. Broulard Collection. A-2; B-1; C-3; F-4; G-1. (See Plate VII)

Fig. P-32. Hunter holding French horn. Freed Collection. C-3; F-1.

Fig. P-33. Laughing boy with dog. Freed Collection. F-2.

Fig. P-34. Laughing girl. Freed Collection. C-1; F-1.

216

Fig. P-35. Girl street musician playing hurdy-gurdy. Brosio Collection, Museo Civico, Turin. T-1.

Fig. P-36. Boy street entertainer holding monkey. Brosio Collection, Museo Civico, Turin. T-1.

Fig. P-37. Breton woman, with a child, crocheting. Newman Collection. C-1; N-1.

Fig. P-38. Breton boy playing bagpipe. Newman Collection. C-1; F-1; N-1.

Fig. P-39. Baker boy. Brosio Collection, Museo Civico, Turin. C-1; F-1; T-1.

Fig. P-40. Cocoa vendor. Georges Berthelot Collection. A-1.

Fig. P-41. Dutch sister holding infant. Freed Collection.
C-1; F-2.

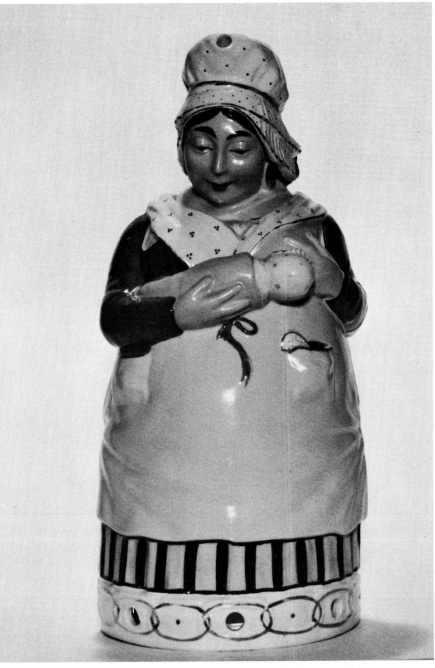

Fig. P-42. Peasant nursing infant. Freed Collection. F-2.

Fig. P-43. Monk carrying wine basket. Newman Collection. A-3; B-1; C-4; F-4; G-1; N-1; T-5.

220

Fig. P-44. Nun holding teacup. Broulard Collection. A-5;
B-1; C-3; F-5; G-2; N-1; T-2.

Fig. P-45. Madonna and Child, with cherubs. Freed Collection. C-1; F-1.

Fig. P-47. St. Vincent de Paul carrying infant. Newman Collection. A-2; C-1; F-2; G-1; N-1.

Fig. P-46. St. Cecilia. Freed Collection. B-1; F-1.

Fig. P-48. Biblical woman, with boy, holding wine jar and bread. Brosio Collection, Museo Civico, Turin. T-1.

Fig. P-49. Oriental sultan. Chiavassa Collection. B-1; C-4; F-2; G-1; N-1; T-2.

Fig. P-50. Oriental sultana. Chiavassa Collection. A-1; C-2; F-3; N-1.

Fig. P-51. Oriental man holding pipe. Brosio Collection, Museo Civico, Turin. B-1; C-4; F-2; G-1; T-1.

Fig. P-52. Oriental woman with bird on wrist. Gandur Collection. B-1; C-4; F-3; G-3; T-1.

224

Fig. P-53. Oriental warrior unsheathing dagger. Brosio
Collection, Museo Civico, Turin. A-1; C-1; F-1; N-1; T-1.

Fig. P-54. Oriental woman playing lyre. Newman Collection. C-1; F-2; N-1.

Fig. P-55. Oriental woman with crossed arms. Gandur Collection. A-1; B-1; C-3; F-2; G-2; N-2; T-1.

Fig. P-56. Oriental woman holding ewer. Brosio Collection, Museo Civico, Turin. A-1; B-1; N-1; T-1.

Fig. P-57. Oriental couple. Brosio Collection, Museo Civico, Turin. C-1; F-1; T-1.

227

Fig. P-58. Zouave holding drinking mug. Freed Collection. B-1; C-2; F-2.

Fig. P-59. Chinese mandarin. Freed Collection. A-1; C-2; F-3; N-1. (See Plate VI.)

228

Fig. P-61. Chinese man, seated, holding teacup. Brosio Collection, Museo Civico, Turin. F-1; G-1; T-2.

Fig. P-60. Chinese mandariness. Broulard Collection. A-1; B-1; C-1; N-1. (See Plate VI.)

Fig. P-62. Chinese woman, seated, holding fan. Freed Collection. C-1; F-2.

Fig. P-63. Elephant squatting on its haunches. Chiavassa Collection. C-1.

Fig. P-64. Elephant, standing, in man's attire. Chiavassa Collection. C-1; F-1.

230

Fig. P-65. Fox with stolen goose. Brosio Collection, Museo Civico, Turin. T-1.

Fig. P-66. Elephant with mahout. Brosio Collection, Museo Civico, Turin. T-1.

231

Fig. P-67. Elephant with howdah. Brosio Collection, Museo Civico, Turin. F-1; G-1; T-1.

Fig. P-68. Camel with howdah. Freed Collection. C-1; F-2; G-1.

Fig. P-69. Teapot in form of duck. Freed Collection. F-1.

Fig. P-70. Teapot with three drinking monkeys. Brosio Collection, Museo Civico, Turin. C-4; T-1.

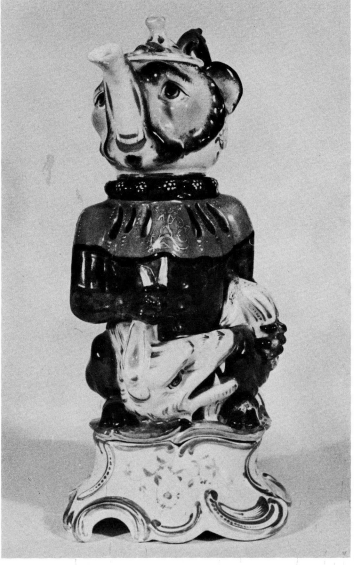

Fig. P-72. Grotesque human. Broulard Collection. A-1; B-1; C-1. (See Plate IX.)

233

Fig. P-71. Grotesque beast. Freed Collection. C-6; F-8; G-1; T-2.

Fig. P-74. Bacchus riding goat. Newman Collection. A-2; B-1; C-4; F-2; G-1; N-1; T-1.

Fig. P-73. Amphitrite riding dolphin. Freed Collection. A-1; C-3; F-2; G-1; N-1. (See Plate X.)

234

Fig. P-75. Triton riding dolphin, with trident. Broulard Collection. A-2; B-1; C-1; F-3; G-1; T-2.

Fig. P-76. Triton riding dolphin, blowing conch. Chiavassa Collection. C-2.

Fig. P-77. Cupid riding dolphin, with birds. Freed Collection. A-1; C-1; F-3.

Fig. P-78. Cupid riding swan. Freed Collection. A-1; C-3; F-1.

236

Fig. P-79. Mermaid. Freed Collection. C-1; F-2; N-1.

Fig. P-80. Woman beside statued commode. Freed Collection. A-1; F-2.

237

Fig. P-81. Woman beside fountain. Brosio Collection, Museo Civico, Turin. C-1; F-1; T-1.

Fig. P-83. Man behind peepshow, with four children. Freed Collection. C-2; F-3; G-1; N-1.

Fig. P-82. Woman seated beside tree stump. Brosio Collection, Museo Civico, Turin. A-1; B-1; C-1; F-4; G-1; T-1.

Fig. P-84. Roman gladiator. Chiavassa Collection. C-2; F-1.

Fig. P-85. Roman matron. Chiavassa Collection. C-1.

Fig. P-86. Nostradamus. René Berthelot Collection, Paris. A-1.

240

Fig. P-87. Bust of Scotsman. Gandur Collection. C-2; F-2; G-1; T-1.

Fig. P-88. Bust of garlanded maiden. Freed Collection. F-1.

Fig. P-89. Princess de Bainviller. Freed Collection. F-2.

Fig. P-90. Girl in crinoline holding a dog. Chiavassa Collection. C-3.

Fig. P-91. Lady wearing riding habit. Newman Collection. N-1.

242

# Notes and References

(References Are Cited in Chronological Order.)

1. Harold Newman, "Reveille for Veilleuses," *Apollo Magazine*, London, February and March, 1955, pp. 35, 71, cited in Reginald G. Haggar, *Concise Encyclopedia of Continental Pottery and Porcelain*, London, 1960, pp. 487, 532; Saint-Cère, "Un Bibelot Romantique: La Veilleuse," *Plaisir de France*, Paris, February, 1956, p. 48; G. Bernard Hughes, "Food Warmers at the Georgian Bedside," *Country Life Magazine*, London, October 31, 1957, p. 930; Valentino Brosio, *Porcellane e Maioliche Italiane dell'Ottocento*, Milan, 2nd ed., 1962, pp. 97-104; John Bedford, *More Looking in Junk Shops*, London, 1962, p. 94; Lura Woodside Watkins, "Food Warmers and their lamps," *Antiques Magazine*, New York, August 1964, p. 174. See also *L'Europeo* (magazine), Milan, January 6, 1957 (Brosio and Chiavassa Collections); *Hobbies Magazine*, Chicago, April 1960, p. 28 (Freed Collection); Amelia E. MacSwiggan, *Fairy Lamps*, New York, 1962, pp. 79-83 (Freed Collection); *Noir et Blanc* (newspaper), Paris, May 22, 1963, p. 341 (Gandur Collection); Michel Saissac, "Les Chasseurs de Tisanières," *ABC Décor* (magazine), Paris, May 1966, p. 33 (Gandur and Berthelot Collections).

2. Hughes, *op. cit.*, p. 930.

3. A fictional reference to *personnages* is made in the novel *Steamboat Gothic*, by Frances Parkinson Keyes, New York, 1952, p. 52. The piece there described is similar to that shown in Fig. P–45.

4. Letter from Mrs. Eva R. Pinto, Northwood, England, to *Apollo Magazine*, London, May 1955, p. 150.

5. *Ibid.*, p. 150, with photographs.

6. Letter from Rex deC. Nan Kivell, London, to *Apollo Magazine*, London, May 1955, p. 150. Photograph is at Australia House, London.

7. *Catalogue of Christie, Manson and Woods, Ltd.*, London, June 13, 1941, lot 161; sale price was £76/14/0. See also *Old Wedgwood* (annual publication of the Wedgwood Club, Boston, Massachusetts), No. 8, 1941, p. 82, figure on p. 100.

8. One brass veilleuse in the Newman Collection bears the inscription, in Japanese characters, on the side of the pedestal and as a part of the etched decoration, "Made by Mr. Takejiro Murakami, Kyoto City, Japan."

9. *Catalogue of Rare Porcelain Veilleuses of Dr. Frederick C. Freed*, Trenton, Tennessee, 4th ed., 1964.

10. Photographs of *personnage* veilleuses from these collections are identified, in the captions of the *Album of Personnages*, by letter as follows (with the number of like pieces in the collection indicated, e.g., B-2):

    Georges and René Berthelot,

| | |
|---|---|
| Paris, France | A |
| Henri J. Broulard, Baumes-les-Messieurs, France | B |
| Nobile Dott. Mario Chiavassa, Milan, Italy | C |
| Dr. Frederick C. Freed, Trenton, Tennessee | F |
| Jacques Gandur, Orléans, France | G |
| Harold Newman, Metairie, Louisiana | N |
| Valentino Brosio, Turin, Italy | T |

11. *The Journal of Hellenic Studies,* London, 1909, Vol. XXIX, p. 164, Fig. 17; *Bonner Jahrbücher,* Bonn, 1909, Vol. 118, Pl. XXXII (6); H. B. Walters, *Catalogue of the Greek and Roman Lamps in the British Museum,* London, 1914, Item No. 1432, p. 217.

12. Manual González Martí, *Céramica del Levante Español,* Barcelona, 1944, Vol. I, Fig. 324.

13. Pompeo Molmenti, *La Storia di Venezia nelle Vita Privata,* Bergamo, 1906, Vol. II, p. 156 (called a *"Lampada (Veilleuse)"*).

14. *Les Arts* (magazine), Paris, September 1914, No. 153, p. 20 (called a *"Veilleuse"*).

15. *Les Arts, supra,* July 1904, No. 31, Fig. 40, p. 32 (called a *"Brûle-Parfum"*).

16. Warren E. Cox *The Book of Pottery and Porcelain,* New York, 1944, Vol. 2, Fig. 805, p. 562.

17. *Ibid.,* Fig. 872.

18. *Ibid.,* Vol. 1, Pl. 71.

19. Henri Havard, *La Céramique Hollandaise,* Amsterdam, 1909, Fig. 111, reproduced from M. de Blegny, *Le Bon Usage du Thé,* Lyons, 1687, p. 34, showing sketches of these pieces.

20. Celia Hemming, "Bristol Delft," *The Connoisseur,* London, August 1918, Fig. XII, p. 219 (then in the Hemming Collection); Newman, *op. cit.,* Fig. II; R. J. Charleston, "Pottery, Porcelain and Glass," *The Early Georgian Period, 1714-1760, The Connoisseur Period Guides,* London, 1957, Pl. 46(D), the caption attributing the piece to the "first half of the 18th century"; Wolf Mankowitz and Reginald G. Haggar, *The Concise Encyclopedia of English Pottery and Porcelain,* London, 1957, Pl. 18(D), with caption as in *The Early Georgian Period, supra;* Hughes, *op. cit.,* Fig. 1

(no date indicated); L. G. G. Ramsey, *Antique English Pottery, Porcelain and Glass,* London, 1961, Pl. 15(D) and p. 33, with same text and caption as in *The Early Georgian Period, supra;* Watkins, *op. cit.,* Fig. 1.

21. Hughes, *op. cit.,* p. 931.

22. W. J. Pountney, *Old Bristol Potteries,* London, 1920, pp. 141, 174, and Pl. XXXIV.

23. *Ibid.,* pp. 10, 153.

24. F. H. Garner, *English Delftware,* London, 1948, p. 25.

25. The quoted captions to the Plates referred to in Note 20 are the only known attributions of a delftware food warmer to a date before 1750. Although it has been said that "English potters began to make pap warmers long before 1750" (Watkins, *op. cit.,* p. 174), the same article says that the piece referred to in Note 20 is "among the earliest of these contrivances" and the caption there gives the date as "c. 1750," with no support whatsoever for the "long before 1750" assertion — unless the operative word is "began."

26. Bernard and Therle Hughes, *The Collector's Encyclopedia of English Ceramics,* London, 1956, Pl. 8.

27. Vivian J. Scheidemantel, "English Delftware," *Antiques Magazine,* New York, December 1953, Fig. 6, p. 466; Dr. T. G. H. Drake, "Pap and Panada," *Annals of Medical History,* New York, 1931, New Series, Vol. 3, No. 3, Fig. 3, p. 292.

28. *Sotheby Catalogue,* London, March 2, 1965, lot 126, with photograph; sale price was £220 (about $616). Also an incomplete piece in combined lot 29; sale price £30 (about $84). *Ibid.,* June 29, 1965, lot 60, a complete but repaired piece; sale price was £125 (about $350). *Ibid.,* October 26, 1965, pedestal only, with mask badly chipped, in combined lot 18; sale price was £50 (about $140). *Catalogue of Christie, Manson and Woods, Ltd.,* London, November 9, 1965, lot 45, repaired pedestal and bowl, incorrectly catalogued as "Lambeth Delft"; unsold at £20 against £25 reserve.

29. Dr. T. G. H. Drake, "Infant Feeders and Feeding in Bygone Days," *The Chemist and Druggist,* Lon-

don, June 30, 1956, Fig. 7(A), showing one of the eight Drake delftware food warmers.

30. *Sotheby Catalogue,* London, May 26, 1938, lot 355; sale price was £6. *Ibid.,* December 6, 1955, lot 31, with photograph; sale price was £25 (about $70). *Ibid.,* July 7, 1959, lot 84; sale price was £40 (about $112). Also, *Connaissance des Arts,* Paris, May 1956, p. 67 and photograph; *Catalogue, Worthing Art Gallery,* Worthing, England, 1957, No. 32.

31. *Sotheby Catalogue,* London, October 31, 1961, lot 34; sale price was £68 (about $190). Piece had been in Levine, Lee, and Willement Collections.

32. *Sotheby Catalogue,* London, January 23, 1962, combined lot 90; sale price was £38 (about $106).

33. A. J. B. Kiddell, "Lowestoft China," *The Connoisseur,* London, October, 1937, p. 185, Fig. XVI.

34. Drake, "Infant Feeders and Feeding," *supra,* Fig. 7(B). The late Dr. Drake wrote the author in 1955 that "about 10 to 15 years ago I saw a base only, of exactly the same design but somewhat different flower decoration, to be sold at Sotheby's."

35. *The Burnap Collection of English Pottery,* Kansas City, Missouri, 1953, Fig. 330; Watkins, *op. cit.,* Fig. 2.

36. *Sotheby Catalogue,* London May 24, 1938, lot 26, with photograph; sale price was £9/10/0.

37. *Antiques Magazine,* New York, October 1964, p. 378, with photograph of one.

38. Drake, *supra,* Fig. 7(C).

39. *Old Wedgwood,* No. 12, 1945, p. 128.

40. *Wedgwood Queen's Ware Catalogue,* 1817, Pl. 15, Design 815. See reprint in Wolf Mankowitz, *Wedgwood,* London, 1953, Fig. 26; *Old Wedgwood,* No. 12, 1945, sketch on p. 127 from the 1838 *Wedgwood Catalogue* and reference on p. 126 to "ceramic food warmers for travelers, nurseries and sickrooms." Also, Watkins, *op. cit.,* Fig. 7.

41. *Wedgwood Queen's Ware Catalogue,* 1817, Pl. 15, Design 815. See reprint in Mankowitz, *Wedg-*

*wood, supra,* Fig. 26.

42. *Wedgwood Queen's Ware Catalogue,* 1774, Pl. 11, Design 57. See reprint in Mankowitz, *Wedgwood, supra,* Fig. 11, and in *Old Wedgwood,* No. 9, 1942, p. 111. Also, Watkins, *op. cit.,* Fig. 6.

43. *Old Wedgwood,* No. 9, 1942, p. 102.

44. *Wedgwood Queen's Ware Catalogue,* 1817, Pl. 15, Designs 813 and 815, engraved by William Blake. See reprint in Mankowitz, *Wedgwood, supra,* Fig. 26. Similar designs (813 and 815) are in *Catalogues* of 1850, 1873, and 1878 at the Buten Museum, Merion, Pa.

45. The design for what may have been a Wedgwood food warmer has been attributed by Eliza Meteyard, *A Group of Englishmen,* London, 1871, p. 264, to Dr. Robert Darwin, son-in-law of the elder Josiah Wedgwood: "Dr. Robert Darwin had a taste for mechanical invention . . . He made a design for a nursery lamp, for use for feeding children. It was in part manufactured at Etruria, and had a large sale." But as the original tea warmer design was printed as far back as the 1774 *Catalogue, supra,* and as Dr. Darwin was then eight years old and did not marry into the Wedgwood family until 1796, any design by him must have been a later adaptation, perhaps the 1817 *Catalogue* pap warmer.

46. *Old Wedgwood,* No. 12, 1945, p. 126, figured on p. 127.

47. Harry M. Buten, *Wedgwood Counterpoint,* Merion, Pa. 1962, p. 250.

48. W. B. Honey, *Wedgwood Ware,* London, 1949, Pl. 21; Newman, *op. cit.,* Fig. III; Hughes, "Food Warmers at the Georgian Bedside," *supra,* Fig. 6; G. Bernard Hughes, *English and Scottish Earthenware,* London, 1961, Pl. 29 (left); Griselda Lewis, *A Picture History of English Pottery,* New York, 1956, Pl. 139 (left).

49. Hughes, *English and Scottish Earthenware, supra,* Pl. 26.

50. Gustav E. Pazaurek, *Steingut,* Stuttgart, 1922, Pl. 9.

51. *Catalogue, Christie, Manson and Woods, Ltd.,* London, June 14, 1965, lot 2; sale price was £27/6/0 (about $75).

52. *Old Wedgwood,* No. 5, 1938, p. 14, figured on opposite page; *ibid.,* No. 8, 1941, figured on p. 100.

53. *Wedgwood First Shape Book* (nineteenth-century reproductions of pages from early catalogues), a copy of which is at the Wedgwood Museum, Barlaston, England, and the Buten Museum, Merion, Pa.

54. *Ibid.,* Fig. 816.

55. *Ibid.,* Fig. 814.

56. *Ibid.,* Fig. 813 (deleted).

57. *Ibid.,* Fig. 811.

58. Brosio, *op. cit.,* Fig. B, p. 104.

59. Byron A. Born, "Josiah Wedgwood's Queensware," *Metropolitan Museum of Art Bulletin,* New York, May 1964, Fig. 5, p. 293.

60. Such a red stoneware piece, with identical marks, has been stated to have been "in 1961 temporarily in the possession of the Victoria and Albert Museum." Robin Price, "Some Groups of English Redware of the Mid-Eighteenth Century, Part II," *The English Ceramic Circle Transactions,* London, 1962, Vol. 5, Part 3, pp. 157, 168. The piece there referred to was in fact sent by the then owner, Mr. Harvard Gunn, to the Victoria and Albert Museum for photographing in January 1958 (not 1961, as stated), in which same year Colonial Williamsburg acquired its red stoneware food warmer at Sotheby's (see Note 64), so that certainly it is the identical piece referred to by Robin Price.

61. Harry Barnard, *Chats on Wedgwood Ware,* London, 1924, p. 67; John Meredith Graham II and Hensleigh Cecil Wedgwood, *Wedgwood,* Brooklyn, 1948, p. 28.

62. Mankowitz, *Wedgwood, supra,* pp. 125-27.

63. Donald C. Towner, *The Leeds Pottery,* London, 1963, p. 24.

64. *Sotheby Catalogue,* London, October 21, 1958, lot 19; sale price was £68 (about $190).

65. G. W. and F. A. Rhead, *Staffordshire Pots and Pottery,* London, 1906, p. 146.

66. *Ibid.,* Plate opposite p. 162.

67. Llewellynn Jewitt, *The Ceramic Art of Great Britain,* London, 2nd ed., 1883, p. 481; W. B. Honey, *European Ceramic Art* (*Dictionary*), London, 1952, p. 474.

68. Drake, "Infant Feeders and Feeding," *supra,* Fig. 7(D).

69. Donald C. Towner, *English Cream-coloured Earthenware,* London, 1957, Pl. 46.

70. Lewis, *op. cit.,* Pl. 139 (right). The Victoria and Albert Museum displays this piece as Staffordshire.

71. Hughes, "Food Warmers at the Georgian Bedside," *supra,* p. 930.

72. Donald C. Towner, *Handbook of Leeds Pottery at the Leeds City Art Gallery,* 1951, Fig. 34 ("Food Warmer – Caudle Pot"); Hughes, *supra,* Fig. 2 (called there a "Food-Warmer"); and G. Bernard Hughes, *Victorian Pottery and Porcelain,* London, 1959, Pl. 21 (same piece called a "Toddy-Warmer.")

73. *Old Wedgwood,* No. 12, 1945, p. 128, describing this piece as "a Queen's ware specimen with foliated rope handles, a stand with more elaborate piercing for ventilation, and a nest of pans or pannikins." The "nest of pans" presumably referred to the bowl and the liner; the reference to "rope handles" and the attribution to "Queen's ware" are erroneous.

74. Hughes, "Food Warmers at the Georgian Bedside," *supra,* Figs. 4 and 5.

75. *Ibid.,* Fig. 3 (right).

76. *Ibid.,* Fig. 3 (left); Hughes, *English and Scottish Earthenware, supra,* Pl. 29 (right). This piece is not marked "Davenport" as erroneously stated by Hughes.

77. Watkins, *op. cit.,* Fig. 5.

78. *Ibid.,* Fig. 8.

79. Hughes, "Food Warmers at the Georgian Bedside," *supra,* p. 931, and letter from Mr. Hughes to the author.

80. Arthur Hayden, *Chats on English China,* London, 1952, Pl. 30; Newman, *op. cit.,* Fig. IV; Mankowitz and Haggar, *op cit.,* Pl. 100(A); Hughes, *supra,* Fig. 7; G. Bernard Hughes, "Earthenware, China and Glass," *The Regency Period, 1810-1830, The Connoisseur Period Series,* London, 1958, Pl. 59(D); L. G. G. Ramsey, *op. cit.,* Pl.

35(C) and p. 66. In the *Catalogue of the Herbert Allen Collection of English Porcelain, Victoria and Albert Museum,* London, 2nd ed., 1923, by Bernard Rackham, this piece is figured (Pl. 71) and is described (Note 432) as a "food warmer"; this is erroneous, as the upper part is a typical teapot with spout and handle, and shows how the two basic types of veilleuses have been confused.

81. E. S. Auscher, *A History and Description of French Porcelain,* London, 1905, Pl. XXI; Frederick Litchfield, *Pottery and Porcelain,* New York, 6th ed., 1953, Color Plate XXV; *Apollo Magazine,* London, June 1949, p. 145; Pierre Verlet, *Sèvres, Le XVIIIᵉ Siècle,* Paris, 1953, Pl. 30; George Savage, *17th and 18th Century French Porcelain,* London, 1960, Pl. 65. This piece has been erroneously designated in the *Wallace Collection Catalogue,* 1920, Item 165, as a "Perfume Burner."

82. Verlet, *op. cit.,* p. 204, refers to three Sèvres veilleuses sold in 1760, one sold in 1762 to Mme. de Pompadour, and another sold in 1768. There is no indication as to the type of such veilleuses.

83. Newman, *op. cit.,* Fig. V.

84. Arthur Lane, *French Faïence,* London, 1946, Pl. 78-A; George Savage, *Pottery through the Ages,* London, 1959, Fig. 38 (b); Watkins, *op. cit.,* Fig. 3 and p. 174, twice erroneously calling this piece "porcelain."

85. Emile Tilmans, *Faïences de France,* Paris, 1954, Fig. 58.

86. *Répertoire de la Faïence Française,* published after the 1932 Retrospective Exposition of French Faïence from the 16th to the 19th Century, Paris, 1933, Vol. V, Pl. Sceaux 16-C.

87. *Ibid.,* Vol. III, Pl. Nevers, 40-A; Roger Peyre, *La Céramique Française,* Paris, 1910, Figs. 158-163, with several detailed drawings.

88. Charles Damiron, *La Faïence de Lyon, Le XVIIIᵉ Siècle,* Paris, 1926, Pls. XI-62 and XIII-70, 71, 74.

89. *Noir et Blanc, supra,* p. 341, with photograph.

90. Newman, *op. cit.,* Fig. VII.

91. Watkins, *op. cit.,* Fig. 4, erroneously calling this piece "English, c. 1785."

92. G. Arnaud d'Agnel, *La Faïence et la Porcelaine de Marseille,* Marseilles, 1912, Pl. XXXI-3.

93. *Ibid.,* p. 359.

94. *Catalogue of the Collection of M. Raymond Allamand of French Faïence,* sold at Nice, April 12-13, 1955, lot 97 and Pl. VIII.

95. Georges Musset, *Les Faïenceries Rochelaises,* La Rochelle, 1888, p. 141.

96. Régine de Plinval-Salgues, "La Céramique Française aux Expositions Industrielles," *Cahiers de la Céramique et des Arts de Feu,* Sèvres, No. 22, Spring 1961, Fig. 15, p. 101.

97. A. Tardy, *Les Porcelaines Françaises,* Paris, 1950, pp. 37, 38, 84.

98. Paul Alfassa and Jacques Guérin, *Porcelaine Française du XVIIᵉ Siècle au milieu du XIXᵉ Siècle,* Paris, 1930, p. 31.

99. Emile Tilmans, *Porcelaines de France,* Paris, 1953, p. 169; Jean Nicolier, "Le XIXᵉ Siécle Français: Céramique," *Collection Connaissance des Arts,* Paris, 1957, p. 72.

100. W. B. Honey, *French Porcelain of the 18th Century,* London, 1950, p. 63.

101. Honey, *European Ceramic Art (Dictionary), supra,* p. 235.

102. Savage, *op. cit.,* p. 176.

103. Comte X. de Chavagnac and Marquis A. de Grollier, *Histoire des Manufactures Françaises de Porcelaine,* Paris, 1906, p. 636.

104. Litchfield, *op. cit.,* p. 117.

105. Tilmans, *Porcelaines de France, supra,* p. 169; Nicole Ballu, *La Porcelaine Française,* Paris, 1958, p. 11.

106. Tilmans, *Porcelaines de France, supra,* Plate on p. 144 (the caption erroneously calling the piece a *"Bouillotte et son bain-marie,"* as there is definitely no *bain-marie*). An interesting caricature of this *personnage* and its subject is a signed *flacon* in the private collection of Alderman Emanuel Snowman, London, made (probably during the same decade) by A. Popoff, Moscow (see Chapter 8); it is modeled and decorated exactly like the French figure, including the costume, hat, and handle, but the figure, instead of a lady with a teapot, is a monkey holding a bottle and a plate of food.

107. Brosio, *op. cit.,* Fig. A, p. 104.

108. Newman, *op. cit.,* Fig. IX.

109. *Catalogue of Paul Martin, Hôtel des Chevau-Légers,* Versailles, April 19, 1964, lot 6 (Fig. P-49), sale price, F. 2,300 (about $460); lot 26 (Fig. P-31), F. 1,600 (about $320). *Ibid.,* October 4, 1964, lot 113 (Fig. P-23), F. 1,500 (about $300); lot 114 (Fig. P-43), F. 850 (about $170); lot 116 (Figs. P-2 and P-3), F. 2,800 (about $560); lot 117 (Fig. P-31), F. 2,000 (about $400). *Ibid.,* February 28, 1965, lot 26 (Fig. P-27), F. 1,350 (about $270); lot 27 (Fig. P-27), F. 900 (about $180); lot 28 (Fig. P-43), F. 500 (about $100). *Ibid.,* October 17, 1965, lot 87 (Fig. P-43), F. 400 (about $80); lot 88 (Fig. P-4), F. 1,000 (about $200); lot 89 (Fig. P-2), F. 1,000 (about $200); lot 90 (Fig. P-3), F. 1,800 (about $360); lot 91 (Fig. P-29), F. 1,700 (about $340). (Add to all prices 16% commission.) *Sotheby Catalogue,* London, December 14, 1965, lot 78 (Fig. P-55), £26 (about $73). *Catalogue of Christie, Manson and Woods, Ltd.,* London, June 6, 1966, lot 72 (Figs. P-59 and P-60), £136/10/0 (about $382). *Country Life,* London, June 9, 1966, figures Fig. P-2, stating, on the basis of the photograph, that it is "almost certainly German (Thuringian)"; this must be incorrect, as no German *personnage* has been recorded and many other examples of Fig. P-2 are known to be French.

110. Plinval-Salgues, "La Céramique Française," *supra,* p. 107.

111. *Catalogue of Hôtel Drouot, Paris, Sale of the Collection of Mme. Emilienne d'Alençon,* July 6, 1931, lots 8 to 134; prices ranged from F. 60 to F. 500.

111-A. *Ibid.,* Fig. on cover.

112. Alfassa and Guérin, *op. cit.,* Pl. 95-b; *Catalogue, Exposition de Porcelaine, Musée des Arts Décoratifs,* Paris, 1929, No. 1723.

113. Brosio, *op. cit.,* Fig. C, p. 104.

114. *Catalogue of Hôtel Chevau-Légers, supra,* May 10, 1964 (Fig. P-72), with photograph; sale price, F. 2,800 (about $560), plus 16% commission.

115. *Catalogue of Hôtel Drouot, Paris, Sale of the Collection of L. Hardy-Thé of Porcelain of Jacob Petit,* February 16, 1931, lot 156, pair of dolphin veilleuses on which are seated, respectively, figures of Neptune holding a horn of plenty and of Amphitrite holding a ewer (Fig. P-73).

116. Brosio, *op. cit.,* Figure on p. 103, attributing this piece "almost certainly" to Neapolitan manufacture, c. 1850, but as to which French origin is not excluded. *Catalogue of Hôtel des Chevau-Légers, supra,* October 4, 1964, lot 112 (Fig. P-74); sale price, F. 2,400 (about $480), plus 16% commission.

117. *Catalogue of Hôtel des Chevau-Légers, supra,* May 10, 1964, (Fig. P-75), with photograph; sale price, F. 2,900 (about $580), plus 16% commission. Also, Brosio, *op. cit.,* p. 102, Fig. D, captioning this piece "probably Neapolitan, 1850."

118. *Catalogue of Hôtel Chevau-Légers, supra,* October 4, 1964, lot 110 (Fig. P-77), with photograph; sale price was F. 2,500 (about $500), plus 16% commission.

119. *Catalogue of Hôtel Drouot, Collection of Mme. Emilienne d'Alencon, supra,* lot 96. An identical veilleuse, but without the figure and base, is in the Freed Collection (*Catalogue, supra,* Item 287).

120. Plinval-Salgues. "La Céramique Française," *supra,* p. 101.

121. Nicolier, "Le XIXᵉ Siècle Français," *supra,* Fig. 9, p. 83; Jean Nicolier, "La Porcelaine de Paris à l'Heure Impériale," *Connaissance des Arts,* Paris, May 1957, p. 76.

122. Brosio, *op. cit.,* Pl. VI.

123. Newman, *op. cit.,* Fig. XIII; *Cahiers de la Céramique et des Arts de Feu,* Sèvres, No. 6, Spring 1957, p. iv; *Styles de France: Objets et Collections,* published by *Plaisir de France,* Paris, 1955, p. 175.

124. Régine de Plinval-Salgues, "Les Schoelchers et la Porcelaine," *Cahiers de la Céramique, supra,* Fig. 7, p. 55.

125. Brosio, *op. cit.,* Fig. D, p. 104.

126. Haggar, *op. cit.,* p. 94.

127. For a general discussion of lithophanes, see G. A. R. Royle, "Lithophanes," *Antiques Magazine,* New York, April 1936, p. 146; Geoffrey A. Godden, "Lithophanes or Berlin Transparencies," *Antique*

*Finder Magazine,* London, September 1963, p. 7; and, as to English lithophanes, Geoffrey A. Godden, *Victorian Porcelain,* London, 1961, p. 195. Lithophanes have been made in several countries. The process was developed at Sèvres under a patent issued in 1827 to Baron de Bourgoing (A. Brongniart and D. Riocreux, *Description Méthodique du Musée Céramique de la Manufacture Royale de Porcelaine de Sèvres,* Paris, 1845, Vol. 1, p. 289, footnote). It was introduced at Meissen in 1828 and was also used at Berlin and other German factories (Honey, *European Ceramic Art, supra,* p. 370; George Savage, *Porcelain through the Ages,* London, 1954, p. 144.) Several English potteries made lithophane under license from the English patentee, Robert Griffith Jones, 1828, who acquired the method from the French inventor (Geoffrey Bemrose, *Nineteenth Century English Pottery and Porcelain,* London, 1952, p. 43). Lithophanes, which are of thin molded porcelain, should be distinguished from *émaux ombrants,* which were made of pottery impressed under pressure, the hollowed portions of which were filled in with enamels of various colors, producing an effect of light and shadow due to the varying depths of the enamels; this so-called "counterpart of lithophane" was invented c. 1844 by Baron A. de Tremblay, at Rubelles, near Melun, France, who until 1858 used the mark "ADT" (Paul Gasnault and Edouard Garnier, *French Pottery,* London, 1884, p. 169). The largest known collection of lithophanes is at the Blair Museum of Lithophanes, Toledo, Ohio, which has over 2,000, including 10 lithophane veilleuses. No veilleuse of *émail ombrant* is known, but lithophane veilleuses bearing the mark "ADT" are in the Blair and Newman Collections.

128. Brosio, *op. cit.,* Fig. on p. 101 (right).
129. Mankowitz and Haggar, *op. cit.,* p. 130; Haggar, *op. cit.,* p. 269.
130. *Cahiers de la Céramique,* Sèvres, No. 30, Spring 1963, photograph on p. 74.
131. *Styles de France, supra,* p. 186.
132. Nicolier, "Le XIXᵉ Siècle Français," *supra,* Fig. 3, p. 73; Jean le Jeune, *Les Anciennes Manufactures de Porcelaine de Basse-Normandie,* Coutances, 1962, Fig. 26.
133. Le Jeune, *op. cit.,* p. 104.
134. *Catalogue of Hôtel Drouot,* Paris, October 24, 1962, lot 18, with photograph; sale price was F. 720 (about $144).
135. *Plaisir de France, supra,* February 1956, p. 48 *et seq.,* with photographs of 15 French tea warmers of the Empire, Louis Philippe, and Napoleon III periods. See also *Catalogue d'Anciennes Porcelaines Françaises et Européens de D. Rechner,* sold at Monte Carlo, March 14, 1926, lot 322, with photographs of 36 tea warmers; *Catalogue of Hôtel Drouot,* Paris, October 24, 1962, *supra,* lots 1-15 and 17, offering 16 tea warmers; sales prices ranged from F. 70 to 310 (about $14 to $62) for conventional pieces, with a nun *personnage* (Fig. P-44)) (lot 19, with photograph) at F. 900 (about $180) and a cathedral (Fig. 42) (lot 16) at F. 750 (about $150), plus 21% commission in each case. For an example of contemporary topical decoration, see Paul Guth, "Tous les Arts Sont Mis 'Au Ballon'," *Connaissance des Arts,* Paris, January 1957, p. 16, with photograph showing a tea warmer painted with an ascending balloon, c. 1830.
136. Emil Hannover, *Pottery and Porcelain,* London, 1925, Vol. 3, p. 185; Cox, *op. cit.,* Vol. 2, p. 671; George W. Ware, *German and Austrian Porcelain,* Frankfurt, 1950, p. 64; Savage, *Porcelain through the Ages, supra,* p. 160; George Savage, *18th Century German Porcelain,* London, 1958, p. 127; Ruth Berges, *From Gold to Porcelain,* New York, 1963, p. 181; Rollo Charles, *Continental Porcelain of the Eighteenth Century,* London, 1964, p. 94. But see W. B. Honey, *German Porcelain,* London, 1947, p. 27, "The (Nymphenburg) forms include a food warmer not found elsewhere."
137. Cox, *op. cit.,* p. 671.
138. Savage, *18th Century German Porcelain, supra,* p. 127.
139. Ware, *op. cit.,* p. 64.
140. Friedrich H. Hofmann, *Geschichte der bayerischen Porzellan-Manufaktur Nymphenburg,* Leipzig, 1921-23, Vol. 3, p. 570.

141. *Catalogue of Cassirer-Helbing, Berlin, for the Sale of the Collection of Siegfried Salz,* Berlin, March 26-7, 1929, lot 444, Pl. XXXIII; sale price was RM 3,610. See also Robert L. Wyss, *Porzellan, Meisterwerke aus der Sammlung Kocher: Deutsches Porzellan des 18. Jahrhunderts im Bernischen Historischen Museum,* Berne, 1965, p. 196 and figure on p. 197.

142. Friedrich H. Hofmann, *Das europäischen Porzellan des bayerischen Nationalmuseums,* Munich, 1908, Pl. 15 and Note 316; Hofmann, *Nymphenburg, supra,* Vol. 1, Fig. 65; M. Olivar Daydí, *La Porcellana en Europa,* Barcelona, 1952, Vol. I, Pl. 175.

143. Ware, *op. cit.,* Fig. 98; Newman, *op. cit.,* Fig. X.

144. *Neuerwebungen der Kölner Museum, 1962,* Cologne, 1963, Pl. 52, No. 143.

145. Savage, *18th Century German Porcelain, supra,* Pl. 85.

146. Honey, *German Porcelain, supra,* Fig. 38; W. B. Honey, *European Ceramic Art,* London, 1963, 2nd ed., Vol. 1, Fig. 160-c.

147. Hofmann, *Nymphenburg, supra,* Vol. 1, Figs. 50b and 66b. These two pieces are not owned by the Bavarian National Museum, Munich, as there stated, but belong to Munich private collectors.

148. Hofmann, *Nymphenburg, supra,* Vol. 1, Fig. 63-b (figuring this piece when it was at Antiquitätenhandlung Lissauer, Berlin).

149. Hannover, *op. cit.,* p. 187.

150. Hofmann, *Nymphenburg, supra,* Vol. 1, Fig. 66a.

151. *Ibid.,* Vol. 3, p. 571.

152. *Ibid.,* Vol. 1, Fig. 63a.

153. *Sotheby Catalogue,* London, October 9, 1961, lot 668 and Pl. XXXI; sale price was £290 (about $810). Also Charles, *op. cit.,* Pl. 34-A; *Apollo Magazine,* London, November 1965, color plate (in advertisement), p. i.

154. Hofmann, *Das europäisches Porzellan des bayerischen Nationalmuseums, supra,* Pl. 15 and Note 316; Hannover, *op. cit.,* Vol. 3, Fig. 297.

155. Hannover, *op. cit.,* p. 185.

156. Robert Schmidt, *Das Porzellan als Kunstwerk und Kulturspiegel,* Munich, 1925, Fig. 49, translated as *Porcelain as an Art and a Mirror of Fashion,* London, 1932, Fig. 72; Newman, *op. cit.,* Fig. XI.

157. Dudley L. Pickman, *The Golden Age of European Porcelain,* Boston, 1936, p. 77.

158. *Noir et Blanc, supra,* p. 341, with photograph.

159. *Catalogue, Christie, Manson and Woods, Ltd.,* London, July 12, 1965, lot 133; sale price was £52/10/0 (about $150).

160. Kurt Röder and M. Oppenheim, *Das Höchster Porzellan auf der Jahrtausend-Austellung in Mainz, 1925,* Mainz, 1930, Pl. 126-d and Note 712.

161. *Ibid.,* Pl. 128-b and Note 714.

162. *Ibid.,* Note 713.

162-A. Jeanne Giacomotti and Pierre Verlet, *Le Musée national Adrien-Dubouché à Limoges,* Paris, 1965, Fig. 48.

163. Savage, *18th Century German Porcelain, supra,* Pl. 96.

164. Friedrich H. Hofmann, *Frankenthaler Porzellan,* Munich, 1911, Vol. 2, Pl. 195-1.

165. Newman, *op. cit.,* Fig. XII.

166. Olivar Daydí, *op. cit.,* Figs. 205, 206.

167. Ware, *op. cit.,* Fig. 157; Savage, *supra,* Pl. 127(a).

168. Newman, *op. cit.,* Fig. XIII.

169. Otto Hauger, *Durlacher Fayencen,* Karlsruhe, 1951, Fig. 47.

170. Eduard Fuchs and Paul Heiland, *Die deutsche Fayence-Kultur,* Munich, 1925, Pl. 81; Konrad Hüseler, *Deutsche Fayencen,* Stuttgart, 1957, Vol. II, Fig. 435 (erroneously placing this piece at the Bavarian National Museum, Munich); *Weinmüller Catalogue,* Munich, October 4-5, 1961, lot 127, Pl. 33 (sale price was DM 3,600); *Weinmüller Catalogue,* Munich, December 5-6, 1962, lot 110, Pl. 10 (sale price was DM 3,100); Ernst Petrasch, "La Manifattura di Ceramiche di Durlach," *Antichità Viva,* Florence, November-December, 1964, No. 9-10, Fig. 1, p. 20.

171. Hauger, *op. cit.,* Fig. 48.

172. O. Riesebieter, *Die deutschen Fayencen des 17. und 18. Jahrhunderts,* Leipzig, 1921, Fig. 248; Hüseler, *op. cit.,* Vol. III, Fig. 515.

173. Newman, *op. cit.,* Fig. XIV.

174. Ernst Zeh, *Hanauer Fayence,* Marburg, 1913, Fig. 128 and p. 170.

175. Honey, *European Ceramic Art (Dictionary), supra,* p. 679.

176. Giulio Lorenzetti, *Maioliche Veneto del Settecento,* Venice, 1939, Fig. 207 and Note 560.

177. Marchese Leonardo Ginori-Lisci, *La Porcellana di Doccia,* Milan, 1963, Pl. XLIII. See *Sotheby Catalogue,* London, July 5, 1966, lot 22, for a porcelain Doccia food warmer pedestal, c. 1780, of similar form, with blue-glazed ground and the molded parts picked out in blue and pink; sale price was £75 (about $210).

178. Bernard Rackham, *Catalogue of Italian Maiolica in the Victoria and Albert Museum,* London, 1940, Pl. 202 and Note 1270, p. 417; Newman, *op. cit.,* Fig. XVI.

179. Francesco Liverani, "Una Maiolica dei Ferniani," *Faenza,* Faenza, 1958, Vol. 44, No. 2, p. 33, Pl. XXI.

180. *Catalogue, Mostra di Maioliche di Lodi, Milano e Pavia, Museo Poldi-Pezzoli,* Milan, 1964, Fig. 145; Armando Novasconi, Severo Ferrari, and Socrate Corvi, *La Ceramica Lodigiana,* Lodi, 1964, Fig. on p. 181.

181. See Note 206.

182. Socrate Corvi and Armando Novasconi, *La Ceramica Lodigiana,* Lodi, 1959, p. 77, mark 13; Armando Novasconi, *Le Arte Minori nel Lodigiana,* Lodi, 1961, p. 139, mark 13; Novasconi, Ferrari, and Corvi, *op. cit.,* p. 294, marks 26 and 31.

183. Novasconi, Ferrari, and Corvi, *op. cit.,* p. 181.

184. Brosio, *op. cit.,* Fig. on p. 98 (right).

185. Newman, *op. cit.,* Fig. XVII.

186. *Catalogue, Mostra dell'Antica Ceramica di Este, 1960,* Este, 1960, Notes 89 and 92.

187. Lorenzetti, *op. cit.,* Note 178.

188. *Ibid.,* Fig. 227 and Note 484.

189. Brosio, *op. cit.,* Fig. on p. 98 (left); *La Terraglia Italiana,* published by the Società Ceramica Italiana, Laveno, Italy, 1957, Fig. 92.

190. Giuseppe Morazzoni, *Le Porcellane Italiane,* Milan, 1960, Pl. 391.

191. Ginori-Lisci, *op. cit.,* Pl. LXVI.

192. Brosio, *op. cit.,* Fig. on p. 101 (left).

193. *Ibid.,* p. 102, Fig. B.

194. *Ibid.,* p. 102, Fig. E.

195. *Ibid.,* p. 102, Fig. A.

196. Newman, *op. cit.,* Fig. VI.

197. Litchfield, *op. cit.,* p. 186.

198. Alexandre Rozembergh, *Les Marques de la Porcelaine Russe, Période Impériale,* Paris, 1926, p. 20.

199. MacSwiggan, *op. cit.,* p. 113, at right of photograph. (The discussion on pp. 79-83, being based exclusively on the Freed Collection, is not entirely accurate, stating erroneously that such pieces "first appeared in 1830" and referring to examples from Far Eastern countries; this latter misstatement is doubtless due to the fact that in the Freed Catalogues the stated place name after each caption usually indicates the place where Dr. Freed's purchase was made rather than the provenance of the veilleuse.)

200. Alexander Borisovich Saltykov, *Russkaya Keramika XVIII-Nachala XX VV. (Russian Ceramics in the XVIII-XIX Centuries),* Moscow, 1952, figure on p. 247.

201. Emanual Poche, *Böhmisches Porzellan,* Prague, 1956, Pl. 64.

202. Siegfried Ducret, *Die Lenzburger Fayencen,* Aarau, 1950, Fig. 36.

203. *Catalogue d'Exposition Vingt Siècles de Céramique en Suisse, Nyon, 1958,* Item 467, then owned by Mlle. Edith Porret, Lausanne.

204. Ducret, *op. cit.,* Fig. 24.

205. *Ibid.,* Fig. 62.

206. *Ibid.,* Fig. 76; also, Siegfried Ducret, "Die Fayencier-Familie Frey in Lenzburg, 1715-1856," *Faenza,* Faenza, 1948, Vol. 34, p. 122, Pl. XXXIII-b. But see Note 183. A letter from Dr. Ducret to the author concurs in the present Lodi attribution.

207. *Anzeiger für schweizerische Altertumskunde,* Zurich, 1921, Pl. I (3); Newman, *op. cit.,* Fig. XV; Rudolph Schnyder, "18th Century Swiss Fayence," *The Connoisseur,* London, November 1963, Fig. 9, p. 159.

208. *Anzeiger für schweizerische Altertumskunde, supra,* Pls. II(13) and II(14).

209. Siegfried Ducret, *Die Zürcher Porzellan Manufaktur,* Zurich, 1958, Vol. 1, Pl. 176.

210. Edgar Pelichet, *Les Faïences de Nyon,* Nyon,

1952, p. 13; Edgar Pelichet, *Porcelaine de Nyon,* Nyon, 1957, p. 107.

211. Eugène Soil, *Potiers et Faïenciers Tournaisiens,* Tournai, 1886, Pl. XIV (7) and p. 444.

212. *Annales de la Société Royale d'Archéologie de Bruxelles,* Brussels, 1931, Vol. 36, Pl. XVIII.

213. Jean Helbig, *La Céramique Bruxelloise du Bon Vieux Temps,* Brussels, 1946, Pl. XV.

213-A. D. Kighley, "Dutch Porcelain," *The Connoisseur,* London, 1939, Vol. CIII, p. 250.

214. *Mededelingenblad, Vrienden de Frise,* Amsterdam, June 1960, No. 19, Fig. 161.

215. *Ibid.,* Fig. 199.

216. Régine de Plinval-Salgues, "La Contribution Française à la Porcelaine Portugaise," *La Revista, Museu Soares dos Reis,* Oporto, May 1961, 2nd Series, No. 2, Fig. 6.

217. Edwin Atlee Barber, *Catalogue of American Potteries and Porcelains,* Philadelphia, 1893, p. 6; Barber, "The Tucker and Hemphill Porcelain Manufactory, Philadelphia, 1825-1838," *The Bulletin of the Pennsylvania Museum,* Philadelphia, April 1906, No. 14, p. 17; Barber, *The Pottery and Porcelain of the United States,* New York, 3rd ed., 1909, p. 135.

218. Barber, "The Tucker and Hemphill Manufactory," *supra,* pp. 22, 23.

219. Barber, *The Pottery and Porcelain of the United States, supra,* p. 143 and Fig. 70.

220. *Tucker China, 1825-1838,* in the *Exhibition Catalogue of the Philadelphia Museum of Art, 1957,* Philadelphia, 1957, Items 290, 406, 519-22.

221. *Ibid.,* Color Plate XI; *Antiques Magazine,* New York, May 1957, figure on p. 464.

222. Harold Newman, "Ceramic Kettles with Stands," *Antiques Magazine,* New York, February 1966, p. 240.

223. Towner, *English Cream-coloured Earthenware, supra,* Pl. 47; Towner, *Handbook of Leeds Pottery, supra,* Fig. 22; Newman, *supra,* Fig. 1.

224. Joseph R. and Frank Kidson, *Old Leeds Pottery,* Leeds, 1892, Pl. 8 and pp. 63, 123; Arthur Hayden, *Chats on English Earthenware,* London, 1909, figure on p. 295.

225. Newman, *supra,* Fig. 3.

226. Mankowitz and Haggar, *op. cit.,* Pl. 53-B; Hughes, *English and Scottish Earthenware, supra,* Pl. 24(2); Newman, *supra,* Fig. 2.

227. Bernard Rackham, *Catalogue of the Schreiber Collection, Victoria and Albert Museum,* London, 1930, Vol. II, Pl. 70 ("Wedgwood") and Note 242 (suggesting "perhaps" Wedgwood or Astbury); *Old Wedgwood,* No. 10, 1943, figure on p. 103 (implication that it is Wedgwood); Hughes, *supra,* Pl. 22(6) ("Wedgwood"); Towner, *The Leeds Pottery, supra,* Pl. 2 and p. 24 (definitely attributing it to Leeds); G. Bernard Hughes, "Stoneware with Eccentric Patterns," *Country Life Magazine,* London, April 29, 1965, p. 1033 ("Leeds"); Newman, *supra,* Fig. 4.

228. Honey, *French Porcelain of the 18th Century, supra,* Pl. 96; Newman, *supra,* Fig. 10. Suspended within the kettle is a bucket-shaped porcelain vessel with a swing handle of brass wire; its function was probably to contain food to be kept warm when the kettle itself served as a *bain-marie.*

229. Emile Tilmans, *Porcelaines de France, supra,* Plates on pp. 138, 139; Newman, *supra,* Fig. 11.

230. Newman, *supra,* Fig. 8.

231. Schmidt, *op. cit.,* Fig. 36; Friedrich H. Hofmann, *Das Porzellan der europäischen Manufakturen im XVIII. Jahrhundert,* Berlin, 1932, Fig. 442 and p. 412.

232. Georg Lenz, *Berliner Porzellan,* Berlin, 1917, Pl. 21 (89).

233. Newman, *supra,* Fig. 9.

234. Ferrand W. Hudig, *Delfter Fayence,* Berlin, 1929, Fig. 193; Newman, *supra,* Fig. 5.

235. *Catalogue, Frederik Muller & Cie.,* Amsterdam, April 27-30, 1909, lot 1062.

236. Jean Helbig, *Catalogue des Faïences Hollandaises, Musées Royaux d'Art et d'Histoire,* Brussels, 1958, Vol. II, Fig. 60; Newman, *supra,* Fig. 6.

237. *Catalogue, Arnhem Faïence, Municipal Museum,* Arnhem, 1961, Figs. 41, 42, 43.

238. W. Pitcairn Knowles, *Dutch Pottery and Porcelain,* London, 1904, Pl. XLVIII; William Chaffers, *The Keramic Gallery,* London, 2nd ed., 1907, Fig. 176; William Chaffers, *The New Keramic Gallery,* London, 1926, Vol. I, Fig. 234.

239. Newman, *supra*, Fig. 7.

240. Helbig, *Faïences Hollandaises, supra*, Vol. I, Fig. 121.

241. Cox, *op. cit.*, Vol. 2, Fig. 1134.

242. Helbig, *Faïences Hollandaises, supra,* Vol. II, p. 133, No. 654.

243. von Karl Frei, *Zürcher Porzellan*, Basel, 1930, Pl. XII; *Das Schweizerische Landesmuseum, 1898-1948*, Zurich, 1948, Pl. 180.

244. Margaret M. Jourdain and R. Soame Jenyns, *Chinese Export Art of the 18th Century,* London, 1950, Fig. 114.

245. It has been said, in G. Bernard Hughes, "Earthenware, China and Glass," *The Regency Period, 1810-1830, The Connoisseur Period Guides,* London, 1958, p. 99, that "tea warmers (were) enameled to match the tea service" (same text in Ramsey, *op. cit.*, p. 66) and in Hughes, "Food Warmers at the Georgian Bedside," *supra*, p. 931, "A tea warmer was often decorated *en suite* with a tea service, but more often it was a separate addition to the tea equipage." However, no English tea warmer, or even a Continental one, has been found decorated *en suite* with a service, and the only known example of any such piece of this type *en suite* is this Vienna coffee set.

246. Hans Meyer, *Böhmisches Porzellan und Steingut,* Leipzig, 1927, Pl. II (4).

247. G. Bernard Hughes, *More about Collecting Antiques,* London, 1952, Fig. 91.

248. Otto Wanner-Brandt, *Album der Erzeugnisse der ehemaligen Württembergischen Manufaktur Alt-Ludwigsburg,* Stuttgart, 1906, Fig. 1243.

249. Jean Nicolier, "La Porcelaine de Paris à l'Heure Impériale," *supra*, Fig. 1, p. 72.

250. J. Folnesics and E. W. Braun, *Geschichte der K. K. Wiener Porzellan-Manufaktur,* Vienna, 1907, Pl. I(2); J. Folnesics, *Die Wiener-Porzellan Sammlung Karl Mayer,* Vienna, 1914, Pl. XIV, No. 63, and p. 81; Hofmann, *Das Porzellan der europäischen Manufakturen, supra,* Fig. 443 and p. 412; J. F. Hayward, *Vienna Porcelain of the Du Paquier Period,* London, 1952, Pl. 15 and p. 203 (calling this urn a "Vessel (Vase) for water or wine" and placing it then in the L. Blumka Collection, New York City); Robert Schmidt, *Early European Porcelain as Collected by Otto Blohm,* Munich, 1953, Pl. 16 and Note 52, p. 57.

251. Folnesics and Braun, *op. cit.*, figured on p. 23; Hayward, *op. cit.*, Pl. 49(d) and p. 211.

252. Yvonne Hackenbroch, *Meissen and other Continental Porcelain, Faïence and Enamel in the Irwin Untermyer Collection,* New York, 1956, Pl. 102, Fig. 160, and p. 169.

253. *Sotheby Catalogue,* London, February 5, 1952, lot 100; sale price was £300 (about $840).

254. *Het Nederlandse Porcelein, Exhibition Catalogue 95 of the Museum Willet Holthuysen,* Amsterdam, 1952, Fig. 26; W. J. Rust, *Nederland Porselein,* Amsterdam, 1952, Fig. 9.

255. *Antiquarian Magazine,* New York, January 1931, p. 19, has a photograph of a similar piece in an advertisement which described the piece as a "China and metal locomotive, c. 1830, used for heating eggnog and other beverages."

256. See Notes 81 and 157, *supra*.

257. Röder and Oppenheim, *op. cit.*, Pl. 126-c and Note 717.

258. Schmidt, *Early European Porcelain as Collected by Otto Blohm, supra,* Fig. 282.

259. Schmidt, *Porcelain as an Art and a Mirror of Fashion, supra,* Fig. 129.

260. Wanner-Brandt, *op. cit.*, Fig. 1014.

261. Lenz, *op. cit.*, Pl. 52 (219).

262. Lorenzetti, *op. cit.*, Fig. 138 and Note 157.

263. Reginald G. Haggar, "Ceramic Cottages," *Apollo Magazine,* London, September 1950, p. 84; G. Bernard Hughes, "Cottages to Scent a Room," *Country Life Magazine,* London, December 5, 1963, p. 1470.

264. Vittorio Viale, *La Raccoltà Ceramica del Museo Civico di Torino,* Turin, Vol. I, Fig. 63 and p. 43.

265. Saul Levy, *Maioliche Settecentsche Lombarde e Venete,* Milan, 1962, Fig. 303.

266. *Catalogue of Hôtel des Chevau-Légers,* Versailles, April 19, 1964, lot 25 (figures identical with Fig. P-35 and P-36); *ibid.*, June 2, 1964, lot 15 (same pieces); with photographs.

267. Hugh Wakefield, *Victorian Pottery,* London, 1962, Fig. 25 and p. 58.

268. le Jeune, *op. cit.,* Fig. 25; Nicolier, "Le XIX<sup>e</sup> Siècle Français," *supra,* Fig. 6, p. 85. For other such *flacons à liqueur,* see *Catalogue of Hôtel des Chevau-Légers, supra,* October 4, 1964, lots 111 and 115, with photographs.
269. *Catalogue of Hôtel des Chevau-Légers, supra,* April 19, 1964, offering several *flacons à parfum* (lots 23 and 24, with photographs).
270. Mankowitz and Haggar, *op. cit.,* p. 8.
271. *The Oxford English Dictionary,* Oxford, 1961, p. 444. For a silver argyll, see Edward Wenham, *Domestic Silver of Great Britain and Ireland,* London, 1931, pp. 67, 68 and Pl. LIV (3).
272. R. G. Mundy, *English Delft Pottery,* London, 1928, Pl. II(1).
273. F. H. Garner, *op. cit.,* p. 19.
274. *Old Wedgwood,* No. 10, 1943, p. 21, figured on p. 20.
275. *Ibid.,* pp. 20, 21.
276. *Ibid.,* p. 113.
277. *Ibid.,* p. 114, figured on p. 41.
278. See reprint in Harry Barnard, *Chats on Wedgwood Ware,* London, 1924, p. 94 and Pl. 3, Design 8; *Old Wedgwood,* No. 9, 1942, p. 111 and Fig. 8, p. 116; *Wedgwood First Shape Book, supra,* Fig. 823.
279. Buten, *op. cit.,* Fig. on p. 16.
280. *Wedgwood First Shape Book, supra,* Fig. 824.
281. W. B. Honey, *Ceramic Art of China,* London, 1945, Pl. 93-b.
282. Cox, *op. cit.,* Fig. 723.
283. *Sotheby Catalogue,* London, March 2, 1965, lot 70.
284. Corvi and Novasconi, *op. cit.,* Color Plate, p. 37; Levy, *op. cit.,* Fig. 184; Novasconi, Ferrari, and Corvi, *op. cit.,* Color Pl., p. 189 (erroneously stating in the caption that it is of "three" parts, thus overlooking the smaller inside bowl).
285. Levy, *op. cit.,* Pl. XXVI; Novasconi, Ferrari, and Corvi, *op. cit.,* Fig. on p. 188.
286. Lorenzetti, *op. cit.,* Pl. XXVI.
287. *Wedgwood Queen's Ware Catalogue,* 1817, Pl. 12, Design 812. See reprint in Mankowitz, *Wedgwood, supra,* Fig. 23.
288. Soil, *op. cit.,* Pl. XI(1) and pp. 375, 411, with erroneous attribution to the seventeenth century.
289. Beatrice F. Powers and Olive Floyd, *Early American Decorated Tinware,* New York, 1957, Pl. 67; Mary Earle Gould, *Antique Tin and Tole Ware,* Rutland, Vermont, 1958, Pls. 207-8 and 211-14.
290. Watkins, *op. cit.,* Fig. 9.
291. MacSwiggan, *op. cit.,* p. 28.
292. Watkins, *op. cit.,* Fig. 11.

# Addenda

1. p. 30. Attention has been called (pp. 30, 47, 145) to the similar modeling of Fig. 3 (attributed to Lambeth delft), Fig. 18 (attributed to Staffordshire), and Fig. 92 (certainly Doccia). The author has recently acquired a grayish-white Doccia porcelain food warmer pedestal, c. 1780, that is identical in form to Fig. 18 and to the Doccia pedestals owned by Marchese Ginori-Lisci and Avv. Alberto Robiati (see p. 140). It suggests that Fig. 18 is probably also Doccia (except for the replacement cover). See the comments on these pieces on pp. 198–99. Likewise, the author has recently acquired a Doccia pedestal with *bleu-de-roi* ground (see Note 177) similar to Fig. 92, but with lion's-head masks above the aperture and on the reverse.

2. p. 69. A unique marked veilleuse of *porcelaine de la Reine,* from the factory of André-Marie Leboeuf, Rue Thiroux, Paris, 1778–90, recently acquired in the Newman collection, has, instead of a bowl or a teapot, a bucket-shaped receptacle suspended within the pedestal, with a brass bail handle, identical to those receptacles suspended in the Rue Clignancourt tea kettles on stands that are described in Chapter 17 and shown in *Antiques Magazine,* February 1966, p. 244, Figs. 10 and 11. It is decorated with characteristic Angoulême sprays.

254

3. p. 78. No *personnage* has heretofore been conclusively attributed to any country other than France. However, there is a porcelain clock made by the Bohemian factory in Slavkov (Schlaggenwald), c. 1850, which is surmounted by a figure of an Oriental sultan similar in form to Fig. P–49. This clock, belonging to the Národní Galerie, Prague, is at the castle at Klásterec, western Bohemia. (Hans Meyer, *Catalogue, Národní Galerie,* Prague, 1955, Fig. 115.) Accordingly, it seems most probable that Fig. P–49 is of Bohemian provenance, as well as Fig. P–53 (an example apparently decorated by the same hand, similarly richly colored and heavily gilt-encrusted, being in the Newman Collection), and so perhaps are some other *personnages,* possibly less ornate ones made at smaller factories and at a later period, c. 1860.

* * *

On a very recent visit to Prague and Bohemia to explore this possibility, there were seen (1) at Prague, at the Museum for Applied Arts of the Národní Galerie, the *personnage* "Lady in crinoline" (Fig. P–90), bearing the impressed mark "C F" and made by Christian Fischer at Pirkenhammer (Brezová), c. 1847–53, and (2) at Castle Klásterec, near Karlsbad (Karlovy-Vary), a pair of *personnages*, the "Chinese mandarin and mandariness" (Figs. P–59 and P–60), made at Schlaggenwald (Slavkov), c. 1840. No other figure comparable to any known *personnage* was found or reported. The Oriental sultan clock figure made at Schlaggenwald may have been copied from a like non-Bohemian *personnage*, or vice versa (the pieces differ slightly in size and modeling), but the three above-mentioned *personnages* definitely establish that *personnages* were made in Bohemia.

4. p. 128. The pedestal of a porcelain food warmer, c. 1780, from Ottweiler, in the Saarland, is in the Saarlandmuseum, Saarbrücken, Germany. Its unique comical masks are of a boy's head, with red hair, protruding upper teeth, and no lower jaw.

5. p. 133. A Ludwigsburg faïence food warmer is in the Württembergisches Landesmuseum, Stuttgart. (Hans Rupe, *South and Central German Fayence from the Legacy of Dr. Paul Heiland, Bavarian National Museum,* Munich, 1934, Item 423.) It has two air vents with shell-shaped hoods and two dog's-head masks, and it is decorated with polychrome floral sprays.

6. p. 145. A maiolica food warmer from Liguria, Italy, baluster-shaped, with two scroll handles and two masks, is in the collection of Marchese Dott. Ambrogio Doria, Genoa. (Giuseppe Morazzoni, *La Maiolica Antica Ligure,* Milan, 1951, Fig. 130–b.)

7. p. 193. The columnar warming urn described in Chapter 17, heretofore catalogued and displayed at the Victoria and Albert Museum, London, as being Swansea porcelain, 1815–22 (and which is identical in form, except as to its domed cover, to the other two warming urns there mentioned and attributed, respectively, to *porcelaine de Paris* and Ludwigsburg), is now considered by the museum as being French hard-paste porcelain painted by one of the London decorators who painted much Swansea and Nantgarw porcelain and as having an English replacement cover (unlike the covers on the other two urns, which are surmounted by a kylix-like cup). Another warming urn of identical form, with an authentic cover and with the mark "FR" beneath a crown, has recently been attributed to Ludwigsburg (*Catalogue, Herman Combé,* Stuttgart, November 9–10, 1966, lot 823, Fig. 22); its painted decoration features a mask on a shield. It would seem likely that all four identical urns were made at the same factory, probably Ludwigsburg, in white with gilt bands, and that two, perhaps three, were decorated elsewhere.

January 1967.

# Index

258